INTERPRETING THE CROSS

Interpreting the Cross

MAX WARREN

Canon of Westminster

SCM PRESS LTD

BLOOMSBURY STREET LONDON

To
PAT and ROGER
in the fellowship
of Christ's Mission

FIRST PUBLISHED 1966
© SCM PRESS LTD 1966
PRINTED IN GREAT BRITAIN BY
BILLING AND SONS LIMITED
GUILDFORD AND LONDON

CONTENTS

Preface

Introduction: The Wisdom of the Cross   9

1   The Good News of God's Anger   11

2   The Cross and our Sense of Guilt   26

3   The Cross and our Sense of Futility   41

4   The Cross and our Fear of Death   54

5   The Cross in our Ministry of Healing   66

6   The Cross in our Ministry of Teaching   81

7   The Cross in our Ministry of Evangelism   96

8   The Cross in the Sacraments of the Gospel   112

Index of Names   1349658   127

Index of New Testament References   128

PREFACE

THE chapters in this book first took shape in response to an invitation from the Archbishop of Cape Town and the Bishops of Grahamstown and Pretoria to give a series of eight addresses to their clergy in September 1965. This was at once an ordeal and a privilege: an ordeal because I was going into a situation of which I had had no previous experience but only a lot of second-hand knowledge: a privilege because wherever the ministers of God's Word and Sacraments are 'under the Cross' in the sense in which they most certainly are in South Africa, it is a very humbling experience to speak about some of the meanings of the Cross of our Lord Jesus Christ.

As will be readily expected, I came away enormously enriched, not only by innumerable kindnesses and the making of many new friends, but by the flood of light thrown on the subject by the discussions which followed the talks and the exciting contributions made by so many.

To those who invited me, and to those who were such patient listeners, I would express my very deep gratitude for all they gave me.

But there are two other acknowledgments I must make. Earlier in the year I spent part of Holy Week at Wells Theological College and there, at the invitation of the Principal, tried out in slightly different form the material in the first four chapters. I cannot be grateful enough to the Principal himself, his staff, and the students for the immensely stimulating discussions which took place, from which again I was the learner. In this way they joined with me in any service I was able to give to the brethren in South Africa.

Finally, and with a very proper sense of appreciation, I would thank my secretary, Mrs Wood, for all the trouble she took over typing my manuscripts.

MAX WARREN

Abbreviations of Editions of the Bible

AV   Authorized (or King James') Version
RV   Revised Version (1881)
RSV   Revised Standard Version (1952)
NEB New English Bible (New Testament) (1961)

References to the New Testament, unless otherwise stated, are taken from the New English Bible Translation.

INTRODUCTION

The Wisdom of the Cross

THIS DOCTRINE of the cross is sheer folly to those on their way to ruin, but to us who are on the way to salvation it is the power of God. Scripture says, 'I will destroy the wisdom of the wise, and bring to nothing the cleverness of the clever.' Where is your wise man now, your man of learning, or your subtle debater—limited, all of them, to this passing age? God has made the wisdom of this world look foolish. As God in his wisdom ordained, the world failed to find him by its wisdom, and he chose to save those who have faith by the folly of the Gospel. Jews call for miracles, Greeks look for wisdom; but we proclaim Christ—yes, Christ nailed to the cross; and though this is a stumbling-block to Jews and folly to Greeks, yet to those who have heard his call, Jews and Greeks alike, he is the power of God and the wisdom of God.

Divine folly is wiser than the wisdom of man, and divine weakness stronger than man's strength. My brothers, think what sort of people you are, whom God has called. Few of you are men of wisdom, by any human standard; few are powerful or highly born. Yet, to shame the wise, God has chosen what the world counts folly, and to shame what is strong, God has chosen what the world counts weakness. He has chosen things low and contemptible, mere nothings, to overthrow the existing order. And so there is no place for human pride in the presence of God. You are in Christ Jesus by God's act, for God has made him our wisdom; he is our righteousness; in him we are consecrated and set free. And so (in the words of Scripture), 'If a man is proud, let him be proud of the Lord.'

As for me, brothers, when I came to you, I declared the attested truth of God without display of fine words or wisdom. I resolved that while I was with you I would think of nothing but Jesus Christ—Christ nailed to the cross. I came before you weak, as I was then, nervous and shaking with fear. The word I spoke, the gospel I proclaimed, did not sway you with subtle arguments; it carried conviction by spiritual power, so that your faith might be built not upon human wisdom but upon the power of God.

And yet I do speak words of wisdom to those who are ripe for it, not a wisdom belonging to this passing age, nor to any of its governing powers, which are declining to their end; I speak God's hidden wisdom, his secret purpose framed from the very beginning to bring us to our full glory. The powers that rule the world have never known it; if they had, they would not have crucified the Lord of glory. But, in the words of Scripture, 'Things beyond our seeing, things beyond our hearing, things beyond our imagining, all prepared by God for those who love him', these it is that God has revealed to us through the Spirit.

(I Corinthians 1, v. 18—2, v. 10)

1

The Good News of
God's Anger

THERE ARE two texts in the New Testament which, taken
together, present us with the spiritual dilemma of our time
and pose the underlying problem which faces those who
would wish to exercise the ministry of reconciliation committed, as we believe, by Christ to his Church. The first text
comes in St Luke, where in a passage of apocalyptic doom
we read of:

> Men's hearts failing them for fear, and for looking after
> those things which are coming on the earth. (Luke 21.26,
> AV)

In the previous verse we read of 'distress of nations, with
perplexity', a notable understatement, most of us would feel,
who live in the apocalyptic situation of today.

But the real dilemma of our time lies precisely in the
parallel truth about the very people whose hearts are fail-
ing them for fear, a truth expressed by St Paul in Romans,
when he says: 'There is no fear of God before their
eyes' (Rom. 3.18, AV). A vast unease in the human
mind, and a vast emptiness which was once occupied by
God—does that not accurately describe our human situation?

Perhaps the major task of the Christian Church in the
generations ahead, if there are to be such, will lie in demonstrating that that vast emptiness was a tragic human illusion,
that God has been there all the time. I use the word

'demonstrate' as defining the Church's task because I am deeply convinced that it will only be as the world sees a community *living* as if God was there all the time and not just talking about God, that it will take the Church seriously. When the world sees what it means to be a 'reconciled community' it may begin to believe in its own need of reconciliation. Then the impersonality of fate may dissolve to reveal a God who must be understood in terms which include the personal and the moral—a God who can be feared precisely because he can be loved.

But within the Church itself there is a prior task, to recover within the Church a new confidence in God derived from a recovery of the Biblical revelation of God in its completeness. Only as we know him in whom we have believed will we become a community with something to reveal, with Someone to reveal.

In what sense are we to understand that it is 'Someone' we have to reveal. In what sense can we say that God is personal?

There is a sound argument which can be built upon the findings of human experience about the value of persons. The depths to which humanity can sink, no less than the heights to which it can rise, suggest that in human personality there is something distinctive in the universe—distinctive at least in the sense that so far no evidence has been produced which challenges this uniqueness. And even suppose that the exploration of outer space does lead to the discovery of persons like ourselves in some other worlds, that would not affect the uniqueness of personality but would simply mean that this particular bit of the universe, our earth, was not unique.

Now we could go on from this to argue, again not unreasonably, that the heights to which men can rise seem to find some correlation with that quality of spirit which we call humility—a willingness to offer oneself not assert oneself.

It would seem, then, that the fact of human personality,

what we call the spiritual value of the person, is something that has to be explained.

By no means dependent on that line of argument yet necessarily related to it is what we think of the Person of Jesus. It is not seriously open to argument that Jesus, the Jesus of the gospels, has been the starting-point of the most fruitful human thinking about persons, about man. The whole manner of his living and dying has had a matchless appeal all down the centuries. That way of living and dying has inspired some of the most exciting adventures of the human spirit. And those who are least willing to interpret the Person of Jesus, as Christians wish to do, are nevertheless wistful in their reverence for him. He is quite inescapable even by those who most wish to escape him.

Surely it is no accident that in Jesus we discern the quality of humility as the very norm by which all humility is to be judged. We need not at this point follow all St Paul's argument in Philippians, ch. 2, but we can respond to the force of his appeal, 'Let this mind be in you which was also in Christ Jesus' (AV), and acknowledge the validity of that as our own aspiration.

This Jesus of whom so much can be claimed without bringing in any Christian theology: this Jesus who was so supremely Man at his highest because Man at the very apex of humility: this Jesus quite deliberately thought of himself and spoke of himself as being dependent not on himself but on Someone else. This Someone he described as his Father. That was how he spoke of God.

To speak of God as Father does not mean that the term Father exhausts the meaning of God. What we can say is that it is an 'image' of God made translucent by Jesus. Quite clearly and obviously Jesus thought and spoke of God as 'personal', as a being with whom it was possible to have a relation as between persons. And those who heard Jesus speaking about God as Father certainly understood him to mean that it was as possible to have a personal relationship with God, to think of him in personal terms, as it was

to have a personal relationship with himself.[1] No one who
knew Jesus, however puzzled they might be about him, had
any doubt that he was a person: even though at the time,
and much more subsequently, they were quite clear that the
term 'person' as we use it was not adequate to cover all the
facts about Jesus.

If one thing is clearer than another about the teaching of
Jesus it is his insistence that God has a personal concern for
us as persons.

> If ye then, being evil, know how to give good gifts unto
> your children, how much more shall your Father which is
> in heaven give good things to them that ask him? (Matt.
> 7.11, AV)

The *a fortiori* argument on the lips of Jesus is a very remarkable testimony to the reality of the personal relationship between God and men. And we need to give this full
value bearing in mind that in the Hebrew tradition the father
of a family was beyond all dispute the focus of creation,
redemption and sanctification for the family. The family
knew itself in the father, was continually kept alive, saved,
by the exertions of the father, fulfilled its divinely appointed
role as the nucleus of human society under the leadership
of the father.

In the earliest Hebrew tradition God is the God of the
father of the family. At a critical moment in his life Jacob
says to his Uncle Laban, 'The God of my father hath been
with me' (Gen. 31.5, AV). At another crisis he says, 'O God
of my father Abraham, and God of my father Isaac, the
Lord which saidst unto me. Return unto thy country . . .'
(Gen. 32.9, AV). And as the generations pass we hear even
more clearly the note struck by Psalmist and Prophet:

> Thou art my father, my God, and the rock of my salva-
> tion. (Ps. 89.26, AV)

> Thou, O Lord, art our father, our redeemer; thy name is
> from everlasting. (Isa. 63.16, AV)

[1] Matt. 11.27; Luke 10.22.

They hear God saying:

> Thou shalt call me, My father; and shalt not turn away from me. (Jer. 3.19, AV)

That most moving book in the Old Testament, the prophecy of Hosea, is built round the idea of God as husband and father of his people. That devastating acted parable of Hosea's own marriage is the earthly but poignant parable used to designate God's relationship with his people. This infinitely loving, infinitely stern, infinitely sad prophetic testimony is the high-water mark of the Old Testament revelation of God as father of his people. All the infinite patience of God is in his appeal as father:

> When Israel was a child, then I loved him, and called my son out of Egypt. (Hos. 11.1, AV)

All this Old Testament background, all this ancient religious heritage of Israel, must be understood as being implicit in the way Jesus used the word 'Father' when he spoke of God.

The evidence would seem to suggest that the highest intuitions of Hebrew religion, endorsed by Jesus himself, point towards the inner core of the universe, its heart, as being that to which we must accord a value which in our human speech is least inadequately expressed by the word personal. And Jesus bids us address the heart of the universe as 'Father' confident that he will respond as a father, at his best and truest, responds.

One word more may be in place in regard to the Hebrew religious heritage which lies behind our Lord's use of the word 'Father' to define God. In Hebrew the verb is the determining part of speech, and never abstract nouns. The Hebrew speaks of divine activity, of God doing things, of God in action. No doubt the apostle was right to summarize the significance of what Jesus revealed by saying 'God is love'. But Jesus said God is our Father, and it was always God in fatherly activity whom he was concerned that men should recognize. And in the supreme physical and spiritual and mental agony of the crucifixion it is to God seen active in forgiveness that he commends his murderers, and to a God actively in control of the whole situation that he commends his spirit. The crucifixion begins with a cry to the Father and it ends with a cry to the Father—to God active in loving.

Here is the very heart of the Biblical understanding of God.

Very properly, theology insists that to think rightly about God we must see him as being in some sense 'beyond' and 'outside' his universe, and yet 'within it'. But so concerned has theology been to insist upon God's 'otherness' that it has always found it difficult to do full justice to the fact of his 'within-ness'. Orthodoxy has generally been happier contemplating the majesty of God than pondering his humility. Historically this has meant a greater stress on the deity than on the humanity of our Lord.

Now it is at this point that many of the most sensitive minds of our generation find that Christian thinking about God is unsatisfying. They are acutely aware of the vastness of the universe, a universe whose dimensions become ever more impossible to grasp. We reel as we think of light years and nebulae containing thousands of suns each a million times brighter than our own sun. A God transcendent to such a universe must indeed be a 'God afar off'. Human language about God so conceived must of necessity use such terms as 'out there' and 'up there', nor is it reasonable to quarrel with the terms. No spatial language can do justice to the realm of spirit. But inevitably a picture is formed in the mind to which modern man finds it difficult to give any intelligible meaning. If he is 'up there' or 'out there' how far 'up' and how far 'out' must we conceive him to be? That may be a silly question to ask, but the fact remains that men ask it and dismiss Christians, and people who use such terms as still living in a pre-scientific age.

There would seem to be a real need for us to dwell very much more on the thought of 'God with us'—that is, to start with the fact of Jesus, and with the Biblical understanding of the Fatherhood of God, and to live and die in the light of this genuine revelation of man and his relation with the spiritual universe. It will be a life of faith. But that, after all, is what the Bible insists that life must be. We must take our stand quietly but firmly on the words:

> No man hath seen God at any time; the only-begotten Son, which is in the bosom of the Father, he hath declared him. (John 1.18, AV)

and

> he that hath seen me hath seen the Father. (John 14.9, AV)

A day may come when with deeper insight into the quality of the universe instead of its quantity men will be able to think of God not so much transcending as transmuting his universe. But that time has not yet come, though we may well believe that the key to such an understanding lies in 'The word made flesh' (John 1.14) who as St Paul says is 'the image of the invisible God' (Col. 1.15).

What has been said so far has been concerned to stress the Biblical insistence on the fact that the God with whom we have to reckon is a God who can enter into personal relations with us, and *not* impersonal ones. That is the essential context within which we have to consider the anger of God, what the Bible more commonly speaks of as the wrath of God.

In what sense can we speak of God as being angry, as giving active expression to his anger? Can we in answering that question go further and make the claim that God's anger is part of the good news of the Gospel?

Let us begin by clearing out of the way one objection which, perhaps, lies at the heart of much thinking about the anger of God. Is there not something fundamentally out of proportion in the idea of God, creator and sustainer of all life, paying the attention of anger to one of his creatures?

Can we, you and I, really presume to think of God being angry with us?

To this there are two answers, at one of which we have already arrived. If God can pay us the attention of love, then he can pay us individual attention. Else the word 'Father' is not a revelation but a misuse of language.

But there is another answer. In Biblical thinking, as in the best modern thinking, there is a solidarity of mankind which is the real foundation of our personal existence. 'No man is an island', as Donne has it. We are all 'joined to the main'. God has his purpose for the whole human race and for individuals within it only as being within it, and never as isolated units. Mankind is a body corporate. The individual only becomes himself, can only be fully himself in relation with his fellows. It is axiomatic to all the best contemporary sociological thinking, as to Biblical thinking, that 'whether one member suffers, all the members suffer with it'. Likewise when 'one member is honoured, all the members rejoice with it' (I Cor. 12.26, AV).

When therefore the Bible speaks of the wrath of God, of his anger, it sees this as a judgment on the body corporate. Yet this wrath is no more impersonal than is the relationship of the individual with the rest of the human solidarity.

This idea of our human solidarity is as fundamental for our understanding of God's dealings with mankind as it is for our understanding of the real basis of human dignity. It is no less fundamental for our understanding of God's work of redemption in which he is both judge and saviour.

We cannot escape, we must not try to escape, we must not wish to escape from this solidarity. And we must accept the verdict of Romans 2.1-5 as being a true summary of our human situation and not just as the conclusion of the devastating picture Paul has just painted in Romans 1. See these verses as but the climax of Romans 1 and we seek to stand outside, to feel morally superior to the corrupt world there portrayed. But Paul will not allow us any such easy escape.

You have no excuse, O man, whoever you are, when you judge another; for in passing judgment upon him you condemn yourself, because you, the judge, are doing the very same things. We know that the judgment of God rightly falls upon those who do such things. Do you suppose, O man, that when you judge those who do such things and yet do them yourself, you will escape the judgment of God? Or do you presume upon the riches of his kindness and forbearance and patience? Do you not know that God's kindness is meant to lead you to repentance? But by your hard and impenitent heart you are storing up wrath for yourself on the day of wrath when God's righteous judgment will be revealed. (Rom. 2.1-5, RSV)

One key to unlock the full meaning of that passage is to remember that the hardness and impenitence of heart which is there condemned is condemned precisely because of its attempt to escape from solidarity. Only if there is an acceptance of solidarity in deserving judgment can we expect to share in the solidarity of undeserved mercy. As the same apostle made clear in the climax to another of his arguments:

in making all mankind prisoners to disobedience, God's purpose was to show mercy to all mankind. (Rom. 11.32)

This Biblical conviction about the essential nature of our human solidarity, about our indistinguishable involvement in a common humanity, is the same in both the Old and the New Testament.

We see then that the wrath of God, his anger, is directed at our human solidarity in evil. And from that solidarity there is no escape by any action of our own. The significance of the Exile in the Old Testament is that it illustrates a corporate judgment: just as we may note that the story of Exodus illustrates corporate mercy. But always this judgment on our human solidarity, whatever its instrument, is to be understood as being a personal activity of God. The Bible is quite unequivocal about this and no understanding of the atonement, of the divine work of redemption, is adequate which reduces the personal activity of God to impersonal forces.

While it is perfectly justifiable, on the best Scriptural grounds, to speak of God working through historic events, that does not make it less the personal activity, and the personal responsibility of God. With the prophet Isaiah we best interpret history when, with him, we hear God say: 'Assyria, the rod of my anger, the staff of my fury' (Isa. 10.5, RSV): with Habakkuk hear God's avowal, as astonishing as anything in the Bible:

> Look among the nations, and see; wonder and be astounded. For I am doing a work in your days that you would not believe if told. For lo, I am rousing the Chaldeans, that bitter and hasty nation. . . . (Hab. 1.5-6, RSV)

and with another prophet overhear God directing Cyrus to fulfil his purposes, even though as we know Cyrus gave all the credit for his victories to Marduk, the high god of Babylon. There is a deep irony in the words of God to Cyrus:

> For the sake of my servant Jacob,
>   and Israel my chosen,
> I call you by your name,
>   I surname you, though you do not know me.
> $\qquad$ (Isa. 45.4, RSV)

Living as we do in our day under the pressure of such tremendous events, the victims as we easily think of purely impersonal economic forces, or of sociological phenomena like the population explosion, it is the more important that we insist on holding fast to Biblical insights and make the act of faith in the personal activity of God, who shapes the ends of human history, rough hew its processes as we will. If we cannot do this with history, how can we expect to do it in regard to God's reconciliation of man to himself, the even greater mystery of the atonement?

But there is yet another dimension to this idea of solidarity which is prominent in the Bible. There is not only a solidarity of humanity, but there is a solidarity of humanity with nature. There is a remarkable passage in Isaiah which has many parallels:

Behold, the Lord will lay waste the earth and make it desolate,
and he will twist its surface and scatter its inhabitants.
And it shall be, as with the people, so with the priest;
as with the slave, so with his master;
as with the maid, so with her mistress;
as with the buyer, so with the seller;
as with the lender, so with the borrower;
as with the creditor, so with the debtor.
The earth shall be utterly laid waste and utterly despoiled;
for the Lord has spoken this word.
The earth mourns and withers,
the world languishes and withers;
the heavens languish together with the earth.
The earth lies polluted
under its inhabitants;
for they have transgressed the laws,
violated the statutes,
broken the everlasting covenant.
Therefore a curse devours the earth,
and its inhabitants suffer for their guilt;
therefore the inhabitants of the earth are scorched,
and few men are left. (Isaiah 24.1-6, RSV)

That is a tremendous passage, the key verse of which runs:

The earth lies polluted
under its inhabitants;
for they have transgressed the laws,
violated the statutes,
broken the everlasting covenant.

The natural order is involved with the moral order. There is a place where the laws of the natural order and the laws of the moral order overlap. The rape of the earth by man's selfishness: the creation of dust bowls: the exhaustion of natural resources without any sense of responsibility: here man involves nature in man's own transgression of the laws, natural as well as moral, the violation of statutes, breaking the everlasting covenant by which man was given dominion in order to exercise it in accordance with the divine will. So nature shares in the judgment on man and man in turn suffers from the judgment on nature. Here is a purposed solidarity. And it is no accident that both in the Old Testament and in the New, God's redemption is seen to be a restoration of the natural world as well as of the world of humanity.

> Instead of the thorn shall come up the cypress;
>   instead of the brier shall come up the myrtle;
> and it shall be to the Lord for a memorial,
>   for an everlasting sign which shall not be cut off.
>
> (Isa. 55.13, RSV)

> They shall not hurt or destroy in all my holy mountain. (Isa. 65.25, RSV)

> New heavens and a new earth wherein dwelleth righteousness. (II Peter 3.13, AV)

—when the everlasting covenant is renewed.

Once grasped of the significance of our humanity's solidarity within itself and with nature, we can begin to see what is the real inwardness of the wrath of God. Many years ago Bishop Stephen Neill published a small book with the title *The Wrath and the Peace of God*. From it comes this short quotation.

> It is hard for us to imagine wrath which is entirely free from the personal elements of malice or vindictiveness, and therefore we misconstrue the wrath of God. But if we express it in other words, His wrath is no more than the clear shining of His light, which must go forth implacably to the destruction of all darkness. The best way to understand the doctrine of the wrath of God is to consider the alternatives.

That alternative is not love; since rightly conceived, love and wrath are only the obverse and reverse of the same thing. . . . The alternative to wrath is neutrality—neutrality in the conflict of the world. . . . To live in such a world would be a nightmare. It is only the doctrine of the wrath of God, of His irreconcilable hostility to all evil, which makes life tolerable in such a world as ours.[1]

Here we can begin to see why the news of God's anger is an essential part of the good news of the Gospel.

But there is still some way to go if we are to enter fully into the blessing of God's wrath. Once again it cannot be emphasized too strongly that the good news of the Gospel is the good news of the personal activity of God. And that personal activity can be mediated to us as persons precisely because in Jesus Christ we see the personal activity of God becoming directly involved in our human solidarity.

When in the Creed, at the Holy Communion Service, we confess that he 'was made man' do we at all realize that our confession means that we are echoing his far more wonderful confession? For in taking our nature upon him, there was much more than a 'becoming human'. In most mysterious words the Apostle Paul says:

> God made him one with the sinfulness of men, so that in him we might be made one with the goodness of God. (II Cor. 5.21)

Here is a new and profounder mystery of solidarity, by which Jesus identifies himself with disobedient and sinful mankind, and makes a perfect confession of our sins. He does this, to quote an old divine, by giving: 'a perfect Amen in humanity to the judgment of God on the sin of man'.[2] This is not something done artificially from outside

---

[1] Stephen C. Neill, *The Wrath and the Peace of God* (The Christian Literature Society for India, Madras, Bangalore, Colombo, 1944), pp. 10-11.

[2] John McLeod Campbell, *The Nature of the Atonement* (Macmillan and Co. 1895), p. 117.

our human experience. Rather in Jesus we see that within our human experience there can be a perfect response of obedience to God's holy will, an obedience persevered with up to and beyond the point at which mankind once more expresses its own disobedience by crucifying its obedient representative. But the Amen has been said and it has been said by Man—Man completely at one with the will of God, a dual solidarity which is itself atonement.

Here is no pacifying of an angry God, as though sin and its punishment could be bought off by an innocent victim being substituted for the guilty. That is to make atonement wholly external and fundamentally unreal. What was wrought out for us men and our salvation by the coming in the flesh of Jesus Christ and by his living and dying, was both a revelation of the human heart, 'deceitful above all things and desperately wicked' (Jer. 17.9, AV), crucifying goodness, and also a revelation of the heart of God which utterly condemns evil but loves the evil-doer even when he is doing evil. In Jesus we do indeed see God at work, exposing evil as what it is, something irreconcilably opposed to good, and at the same time exposing himself as loving men to the uttermost, precisely in and through his un-quenched anger with that evil in man which unfits man for that solidarity with God which has all along been God's purpose for man.

Archbishop Temple has this comment on those solemn words in John 3.36, 'The wrath of God abideth on him':

Terrible words. A sentimental and hedonist generation tries to eliminate 'wrath' from its conception of God. Of course, if 'anger' and 'wrath' are taken to mean the emotional reaction of an irritated self-concern, there is no such thing in God. But if God is holy love, and I am in any degree given to uncleanness or selfishness, then there is, in that degree, stark antagonism in God against me. And so long as I am disobedient that *wrath of God* continues.[1]

[1] William Temple, *Readings in St John's Gospel* (Macmillan and Co. 1939), Vol. I, p. 56.

It is the wrath of the personal love of God for me as a person, the wrath without which there would be no good news that 'God so loved the world, that he gave his only begotten Son, that whosoever believeth in him should not perish, but have everlasting life' (John 3.16, AV).

2

The Cross and our Sense of Guilt

THERE IS an old 'Mission' hymn whose opening lines run like this:

> Jesus, I will trust Thee,
> Trust Thee with my soul,
> Guilty, lost, and helpless,
> Thou canst make me whole.

'Guilty, lost, and helpless': we of this second half of the twentieth century are not quite sure what to make of those words. Popularly understood, or misunderstood, the researches of psycho-analysts seem to absolve us of guilt, putting the blame, if anywhere, on our parents or our circumstances. And there is much in our mood which welcomes this escape. With the same alacrity with which Adam blamed Eve and Eve blamed the serpent we also are always on the look-out for some escape clause in the contract of life's responsibilities.

On the other hand we may seek for shelter in a half-misunderstood psychological word like 'complex', finding a brief satisfaction in being the innocent victims of a determination outside our control. Yet, deep in our own selves we retain an uneasy sense that to talk about our complexes as an excuse for a failure of responsibility is essentially playing with words, another evasion of what we know to be true. For we all do in fact act upon the hypothesis that we are free, free to assent or dissent at any moment from this course of action or that, however predisposed we may be by past thought and practice to make one choice rather than the other.

A modern writer, Eric Fromm, in that very searching study of his, *The Fear of Freedom*, throws light on our problem when he describes modern man's plight as being that he feels 'isolated, alone and afraid'. Every nation in our world today, after one fashion or another, is haunted by this sense of being alone. The international world of our time is a jungle and fear stalks through it. And in this respect the nations are but their individual citizens writ large.

The more we ponder those words 'isolated, alone and afraid' the more are we aware of how closely they correspond to the words of that hymn 'Guilty, lost and helpless', with this difference that the hymn could speak of an object of trust. The horror of being 'isolated, alone and afraid' lies precisely in being entirely on our own because there is no one we can trust.

We may claim then that neither shifting the blame on to our parents or to circumstances, to environment or upbringing, nor an over-easy familiarity with psychological jargon, really sets men's minds at ease. In a mood far other than the airy fancies of Shakespeare's *A Midsummer-Night's Dream* we ask:

> Is there no play
> To ease the anguish of a torturing hour? (Act V, sc. 1, lines 36, 37)

The same Shakespeare in more serious mood in *Hamlet* provides us with an answer. We hear the distraught Prince of Denmark clutching at an idea which may be the means of exposing his father's murderer:

> I have heard (he says)
> That guilty creatures sitting at a play
> Have by the very cunning of the scene
> Been struck so to the soul that presently
> They have proclaimed their malefactions.
>
> (Act II, sc. 2, lines 625f.)

Christians believe that the great drama of redemption has had one supreme moment of focus when men watched Christ upon the Cross. More than that, Christian experience insists that that moment moves down time, is strictly speaking contemporaneous, and that by the very cunning of that scene men and women can still be so struck to the soul as to discover the real measure of their guilt.

That, however, must be the conclusion of our argument. First we need to prepare for that 'play' by looking closely at the nature of guilt. For only after understanding what guilt is, and what it is not, can we enjoy the full meaning of what forgiveness is.

At the outset let us accept the universality of the feeling of guilt. No man lacks it, however he may try to rationalize it. Shame itself is one expression of it. Uneasiness is a closely related manifestation. Accepting it then as something with which we are all familiar, it may help to clear our minds if we turn first to consider some of those feelings of guilt which point not so much to an awareness of positive evil in ourselves as to some but half-apprehended good, to that sense of something missing which is so often a challenge to a high spiritual endeavour.

We think, for instance, of that very generous emotion which can make a man genuinely conscience-stricken at his good-fortune when some privilege comes his way which he has in no sense deserved, while others far more deserving are overlooked. The enjoyment of privilege can and does lead many people to a real sense of guilt. 'I am not worthy, Lord', is a genuine response to an unexpected privilege. Equally often, such a sense of having far more than one has ever earned has sent many a man or woman to give un-calculating service to those less fortunate than themselves. There is no mistaking the fact that the more sensitive a person is the more the enjoyment of privilege carries with it a sense of guilt.

Somewhat akin to this unease at an undeserved privilege is that sense of solidarity with those who suffer, with those who are 'outside', which, in the case of Simone Weil, made her resolve not to cross the threshold of the Church lest she should somehow find herself enjoying a spiritual privilege which might separate her from those with whom she wished to identify herself. It is easy to dismiss such a scruple as morbid. Yet there is a nobility here we cannot but admire. Here is a sense of guilt leading to identification with those in need. Comparable to this is the case of some of the noblest Jews of our time who have been completely convinced of the truth about Jesus Christ and give to him their personal allegiance, but feel they cannot accept baptism and so appear to betray their fellow Jews who have suffered so much. Here is a most complex form of guilt, yet one which compels our respect. Again well known is the motive which kept Dr Albert Schweitzer for over fifty years in a West African backwater solely because of his identification with the guilt of Europe in its involvement in the slave trade.

Our Lord, in one of his best known parables, that of the Sheep and the Goats in Matthew, ch. 25, points to an aspect of the Last Judgment which is easily overlooked. It will be the things left undone which will be as much part of the indictment as any wrong actions committed. And there is that other word of our Lord in Matthew, ch. 5, vv. 23-24:

> . . . if thou bring thy gift to the altar, and there rememberest that thy brother hath ought against thee; leave there thy gift before the altar, and go thy way; first be reconciled to thy brother, and then come and offer thy gift. (AV)

Here, if we will, is the divine *imprimatur* on constructive guilt.

Nor is this by any means all that is implicit in this parable of Jesus. For here we are reminded that God expects from us far more than any conventional view of duty demands. If we allow our sensitiveness to the world's suffering to be blunted by familiarity—and we all do allow that to happen —we belong by right to those who at the Last Judgment will find themselves on the Judge's left hand. With this may be listed all those uncomfortable demands of our Lord about 'going the second mile', 'turning the other cheek', surrendering coat as well as cloak. At the end of all our best endeavours we remain 'unprofitable servants: we have done that which was our duty to do' (Luke 17.10, AV). We are one in the community of guilt. That is the only possible starting-point from which to understand our real situation. The end of ourselves is the place for a new start. Hope begins to be possible when in ourselves there is nothing left to hope for. That is the fundamental truth behind the lines:

> Nothing in my hand I bring,
> Simply to thy Cross I cling.

All this points us to a further truth foreshadowed in that remarkable passage in Exodus, ch. 28, where the very insignia of holiness, upon the mitre on Aaron's head, is there to remind him and those who see him that he is bearing 'the iniquity of the holy things, which the children of Israel shall hallow in all their holy gifts' (v. 38, RV). The Revised Standard Version makes the point clearer still when it reads 'Aaron shall take upon himself any guilt incurred in the holy offering which the people of Israel hallow as their holy gifts.' And the passage ends with the words, 'it shall always be upon his forehead, that they may be accepted before the Lord'. This represents the frank acceptance of the fact that our very recognition of goodness is a perpetual reminder of how far we are from being good. Paul Tournier, to whose book *Guilt and Grace* I would acknowledge my profound gratitude, has this formidable sentence:

> . . . the high drama of evil is that it cannot be localized, that it penetrates into the virtues so that there is some evil within the good, so that at least in great measure it is pride which makes us virtuous.[1]

[1] Paul Tournier, *Guilt and Grace* (Hodder and Stoughton 1962), p. 130.

The recognition of an all-pervading guilt is the beginning of realism about oneself, about society, about the nation, about the world—and about the Church.

One further point remains which is relevant to this part of our discussion. Paul Tournier speaks of:

> Guilt at the unfinished, the relative, the failure to develop, the talents lying fallow; guilt at a certain betrayal of oneself, one's aspirations, convictions and human vocation.

Do we not all know this after one fashion or another? Sir Francis Drake once wrote:

> There must be a begynning of any great matter, but the continewing until the end untyll it be thoroughly finished yeldes the true glory.

All these points about 'constructive guilt', which show the sense of something lacking, are indeed a witness to a fundamentally right attitude to life. 'Man partly is and wholly hopes to be,' said Browning. Our very awareness of incompleteness and our acceptance of responsibility for being incomplete, but not content to remain so, is itself a witness within our spirits of the creative Spirit of God. God has 'set eternity in our hearts' and the yearning for eternity is itself prompted and made conscious by our sense of guilt. Here, in part at least, is the tremendous appeal of the Cross, a profound awareness that our deepest yearnings have indeed been felt in heaven. Only completeness can match the need of incompleteness.

The emphasis on what is here called 'constructive guilt' has been put first by way of contradicting the common fallacy, propagated by some types of psychology, and even more by some misunderstandings of psychology, that the sense of guilt if not morbid is at least infantile, something out of which a person is meant to grow. Guilt is a far too complex factor in human life to be dealt with so easily. Let us be bold to say that a sense of guilt is a measure of health. It is indeed 'a driving force toward healing'.[1] It corresponds

[1] Paul Tournier, op. cit., p. 129.

in the spiritual life to the rôle played by pain in our physical experience, the warning that something is wrong and needs attention.

We must now turn to consider a form of guilt which far from being a 'driving force towards healing' is more likely to be a driving force toward despair. This is that sense of guilt which projects itself upon the other who has been wronged, whether that other be a human being or God. This form of projection does not attempt to mitigate the guilt but rather assumes that, as a result of the guilty deed, the one who has been injured or wronged or disobeyed has ceased to love. Such a guilty feeling creates fear, a fear which can lead to hopeless despair or to desperate attempts by the guilty to reinstate himself with the one who is supposed no longer to love him.

Psychologists have shown us through psycho-analysis how widespread is this guilt-ridden conviction that we live in a loveless world. What is not so often noticed is that whole theologies have been constructed upon the assumption that God did not love the world, but had to be persuaded to do so. This is written deep into the long record of man's attempt to come to terms with the God about whom he feels guilty. Back of all the long story of sacrifice lies the assumption that God has to be persuaded to be loving. The very term 'satisfaction' as we have it in the Prayer of Consecration in the Book of Common Prayer hints at this idea, as does that most unfortunate translation in the 4th Comfortable Word—'If any man sin, we have an Advocate with the Father, Jesus Christ the righteous; and he is the propitiation for our sins.'[1] Except to the very well-instructed those words conjure up the idea of a law court with the suggestion of the guilty having had to pay some fine by which justice could be placated. It is indeed a great pity that we cannot straightway adopt the New English Bible rendering and let

[1] The misleading character of this rendering has been clearly pointed out by C. H. Dodd in *The Epistle to the Romans* (Hodder and Stoughton 1932), pp. 54, 55, 60, 61.

THE CROSS AND OUR SENSE OF GUILT   33

the 4th Comfortable Word read 'should anyone commit a sin . . . Jesus Christ . . . is the remedy for the defilement of our sins.' For the very heart of the Gospel lies in the fact that God has never stopped loving us. At the moment when we are most aware of our guilt, most overwhelmed by the evil in ourselves, we are bidden by the Gospel to look at Christ on the Cross. Really to look at him there and to understand why he is there is to be safeguarded from any thoughts of 'cheap grace', of any minimizing of the reality of our guilt. But it is also to know that the last word about our human condition, God's last word to man in man's uttermost extremity, is a word of love.

The hell of guilt is guilty fear, the fear that there cannot be such a thing as real forgiveness, or if forgiveness is possible then we must do something to deserve it. From which cardinal error springs all moralistic religion, all those legalisms that take the sunshine out of life. 'Christ died for us while we were yet sinners, and that is God's own proof of his love towards us' (Rom. 5.8). The Cross is the symbol of the divine anticipation of our guilt. It is in our very guiltiness, in the very midst of our sinning, at the point where in practice we have said 'evil be thou my present good', it is there Christ gives himself for us and to us. Far from our having to do anything to turn God's love back to us we have been enveloped by that love even when we were in the act of sinning. This is what the Apostle means when at the end of the same chapter he writes 'Where sin was thus multiplied, grace immeasurably exceeded it' (v. 20).

We may sum up this part of our argument by saying that it is a true sense of guilt which acknowledges that we are unloving, that we sin against love. But it is a false sense of guilt which says that we are unloved.

At this point in our argument it is perhaps worth noting that we are concerned with a principle of very much wider relevance than the purely personal, deeply relevant as this is for every person. There is, for instance, on the part of Western man a very deep feeling of guilt towards the under-

B

privileged peoples of the world. We may particularize and say that a very large part of the mood in Britain since World War II, which has not only accepted but has welcomed the liquidation of empire, has not been caused primarily by a loss of nerve as some suggest. We may admit that there has been an element of this. But let us also recognize that in part it has been due to our deprivation of the source of material power through the sheer exhaustion of our material resources. We cannot any longer act as an imperial power because the ratio between our capacity for power, and the relative lack of power of other nations has changed radically. Macmillan's famous speech on 'The Wind of Change' can be traced back to the recognition of this change in the actual realities of power in the world.

At this point we face the question, 'Can Britain go on to see that this change in the power structure of the world is a good thing? Can the people of Britain see that the setback to our pride as a conquering, ruling power may bring us to a discovery of ourselves, a recognition of the false gods we were worshipping, and a rediscovery of the true God, and so to a renaissance?' Britain is used here only to illustrate a political principle. For if one thing is certain it is that the whole power-structure of the world as it was in 1939 and in 1945 has been transformed, and is in the process of even greater transformation. The underlying factor of our human situation viewed in global terms is the complete interdependence of mankind. If we continue to think in terms of power as the ultimate reality in human relationships we are bound to arrive at an annihilating war.

In a word, Western man, in Britain and elsewhere, has been awoken to his guilt in regard to his brethren. That the awakening has been due to political rather than religious reasons does not alter the fact that there has been an awakening. Western man still fights against this awareness, but his conscience has been so stabbed into consciousness that he cannot be easy any more. Can this man, this corporate man of the West, see that in being humbled, in accepting the truth about his guilt, he can find the meaning of salvation? There is such a thing as corporate salvation. There is all too general a tendency among Christians to think of salvation in purely personal terms, to treat the atonement as being essentially a device by which the individual can be restored to a right relationship with God, that the guilt of the individual may no longer be a barrier to the peace which God gives him. Of course salvation does mean this. Of course the atonement is an act of God by which the individual is brought home from what he thought was a far country. But this is to take far too limited a view of grace and of the purposes of God. The perspective of the Bible is something far grander. In the Old Testament and in the New the peace of God has a meaning for the entire universe. There is to be a summing up of all things in Christ. God's hidden purpose is:

> that the universe, all in heaven and on earth, might be brought into a unity in Christ. (Eph. 1.10)

The vision of the prophet is that: **1349658**

> they shall beat their swords into ploughshares,
> and their spears into pruning hooks;
> nation shall not lift up sword against nation,
> neither shall they learn war any more.
>
> (Isa. 2.4, RSV)

And the vision of the Seer of the Apocalypse shows us a city the light of which is the glory of God and:

> By its light shall the nations walk; and the kings of the earth shall bring their glory into it . . . they shall bring into it the glory and the honour of the nations. (Rev. 21.24-26, RSV)

Interpret these anticipations how you will, they clearly speak of an atonement, a realization of the divine purpose which is infinitely larger and more comprehensive than the redemption of an elect remnant of fortunate individuals. Nor is it readily possible to read the Epistle to the Ephesians

and what it has to say about the Church; to understand the
great historical retrospect of the Epistle to the Hebrews;
to hear St Paul in his letter to the Romans insist that 'God's
act of grace is out of all proportion to Adam's wrong doing'
(Rom. 5.15); and not to sense the corporate character of
salvation.

All this is the more important because, to perhaps a
deeper degree than was felt by some earlier generations, we
are acutely conscious of the corporate guilt in which we are
all caught up. Not for one single moment of one single day
are we outside the action of the world's evil. No one of us
can pretend an immunity to the 'world's slow stain'. This
we know in the depth of our being. In a very special way
there is an inwardness to our cry even as individuals:

> Miserable creature that I am, who is there to rescue me out
> of this body doomed to death? (Rom. 7.24)

And the more sensitive we are to the realities of life the
more that 'body doomed to death' is seen as the body of
mankind. How truly Donne spoke for us:

> No man is an *Island*, entire of itself. . . . I am involved in
> mankind.

We must be saved together or we will not be saved at all.
That would seem to be the deepest truth about the atonement, a profoundly mysterious truth, not wholly congenial
to our natural self-centredness, but lying as it were somewhere near the base of the whole structure of divine revelation. The Bible is a book about Man and not about individual men, except in so far as they show us Man in his
infinite need and Man as the object of God's infinite grace.

This is why the Old Testament points forward very
mysteriously to a figure of a coming One who more and more
approximates to Man writ large. Indeed it is not always easy
to distinguish between corporate Man and the Man unique,
as any student of the Servant Songs of Isaiah will know. And
the figure in the book of Daniel, 'coming to the Ancient of

Days', is on no common-sense reckoning some individual standing six feet in height. He is the Son of Man. He is the epitome of mankind. He is, as the context suggests, 'The Saints of the Most High'—a corporate designation whose fuller significance emerges in the New Testament as Christ the head of his Body which is the Church, but more than that, much more than that, Christ the second Adam, the fountain head of a redeemed and re-created humanity.

Now it is within this body of ideas and nowhere else that we have to understand the tremendous insistence of the Bible on the corporate nature of the atonement.

> When anyone is united to Christ, there is a new world—*a new act of creation.* (II Cor. 5.17)

The whole suggestion of those words is to take us back in imagination to the time of the beginning, to God's purpose in creation, to Adam, that is to say to Man. To be united to Christ is to become part of Man as God meant Man to be. So it is that with great boldness at the end of the same chapter, as we have seen earlier, St Paul can dare to say: 'God made him one with the sinfulness of men.' Do not let us in the presumption of ignorance pretend that we can fathom the full meaning of those words, any more than we can possibly enter into the full darkness which surrounds the Cross on Calvary. Here indeed *omnia exeunt in mysterium*. Very dimly in rare moments, perhaps in sharing someone's grief at some tragic betrayal of the best they know, we, conscious of our own frailty, feel with them, are hurt by their hurt, know their sin as our own sin. But even in our deepest moments of self-identification with another's need we feel acutely that there is a perfection of insight into their condition, a depth of sympathy and comparison which is beyond our resources. Only someone who, tempted in all points like as we are, sharing in our involvement in the guilt of our world, yet uncorrupted by it, can match that individual's need. And that someone's capacity to meet such need can be inexhaustible only if he comes to us from God.

'God was in Christ reconciling the world unto himself'
(II Cor. 5.19, AV), or as the New English Bible margin has
it, 'God was reconciling the world to himself by Christ'. 'By
Christ'—those words in their full New Testament significance have a twofold significance. Christ is indeed the Son
of Man; he is Man the epitome of Mankind. In Christ is the
new creation, the new order, paradise regained. In another
sense he is a personal saviour. We must always hold on to
this twofold nature of the Christ, a hypostatic union different
from that confessed in the Nicene creed, but not in any way
contradictory of it. He is the 'supreme head to the Church'
so that we can rejoice to be, in the happy rendering of the
New English Bible, 'believers incorporate in Christ Jesus'
(Eph. 1.1). But he is also 'the Son of God who loved me
and sacrificed himself for me' (Gal. 2.20).

Because it remains true that, normally, we feel our
individual guilt most personally, a thought here may be
added about the value we must give to the word 'sacrifice' in
that verse. For only as we give it its full meaning will we see
how it fully matches our guilt. In his book, *The Cruciality of
the Cross*, P. T. Forsyth has a comment which seems to
bring us near to this full meaning. He writes:

> The essential thing was not self-sacrifice, . . . but sacri-
> fice of the central self—not sacrifice by self but of self, and
> of the whole self, sacrifice not merely voluntary but personal,
> loving and entire.[1]

This self-offering of Christ—the complete response of his
total being in holy obedience to the will of God—was something he did for me. It is not just that he did it 'instead of
me'. No one can, in the profoundest sense, ever take
another one's place. Our inherent individuality is too complete for that. Nor is it at all adequate to say that he did it
'on behalf of me', some kind of external transaction. We
come most near to the truth if we see him like the Father in

[1] P. T. Forsyth, *The Cruciality of the Cross* (Independent Press,
2nd Edition 1948), p. 87.

the story of the Prodigal Son at the moment when he embraced his son, took him in his arms, was at-one to him.

Of course no words can really describe this profound experience of ' being found in him'. What is quite certain is that it is something utterly remote from semantic arguments about the significance of Greek prepositions in the language of the New Testament. P. T. Forsyth, in that same book, has a passage which can sum all this up:

> We can no longer treat the atonement as a deflection of God's anger, as if a flash fell on Christ and was conducted by Him to the ground, while we stood in passive safety, with no part or lot in the incomprehensible process. We can no longer speak of a strife of attributes in God the Father, justice set against mercy, and judgment against grace, till an adjustment was effected by the Son. There can be no talk of any mollification of God, or any inducement whatever, offered by either man or some third party, to procure grace. Procured grace is a contradiction in terms. The atonement did not procure grace, it flowed from grace. What was historically offered to God was also eternally offered by God, within the Godhead's unity. The Redeemer was God's gift.[1]

Over against that understanding of the action of Christ crucified, of God in Christ on the cross, let us set the reality of ourselves. And here a quotation from H. R. Mackintosh's book, *The Christian Doctrine of Forgiveness,* may meet our need for understanding:

> To look at the Holy One with realizing mind is to become aware that there is in us an impurity and impotence for which we are answerable. The paradox confronts us; because we are answerable, there can be for us no excuse, yet because we *are* answerable, and sin has not merely happened to us as an infection might, it is possible for us to be forgiven. Only guilty sin can be pardoned; there has taken place a disturbance of our personal relationship to God, and this he can rectify. Indeed, the sense of guilt is of itself a token of hope; it proves we are not hopelessly lost to goodness,

[1] P. T. Forsyth, op. cit., pp. 40-1.

because our eyes are not fast closed to the reality of God. Willingness to accuse ourselves is evidence that he has not wholly forsaken us.[1]

We may then with confidence turn back to where we began and echo the words:

> Jesus, I will trust Thee
> Trust Thee with my soul,
> Guilty, lost, and helpless   .
> Thou canst make me whole.

But we will not stop there. For this is a very great salvation in which we share with that great multitude which no man can number. And beyond even them we look for a new heaven and a new earth in which dwelleth righteousness. No longer separated in our guilt we are no longer 'isolated, alone and afraid'.

[1] H. R. Mackintosh, *The Christian Experience of Forgiveness* (Nisbet 1930), p. 66.

3

The Cross and our Sense
of Futility

WE HAVE seen that a sense of guilt, interpreted widely, is
a universal human experience. Self-awareness, whenever
such a moment of perception comes to us, leaves us in no
doubt about this. But we are adept at avoiding too many
of these moments of real self-awareness. A sense of guilt
may be a universal human experience, but it is certainly
not an ever-present one.

On the other hand, for multitudes of people there is a
very real sense of futility which colours all their living,
influences all their thinking, and has a paralysing effect
upon their wills. Nor can any of us presume to stand outside
this multitude, detached observers of a mood we do not
share. It must be a singularly unimaginative mind which,
confronted by the vast impersonal forces which operate upon
the world of human life, does not know the sense of personal insignificance which suggests the futility of all human
endeavour.

The ancient world spoke of 'fate'. The Muslim has called
it *kismet*, the Hindu *karma*, the Buddhist 'the wheel of
becoming'. All of these were attempts to rationalize either
the apparent indifference of the natural order and its carelessness of the individual life, or to show how small a part
the individual could play in regard to his own destiny. Not
so very different is the common response of contemporary
man to the threat of nuclear destruction, to the apparent loss
of all sense of conscious direction in the field of international

politics, to the certain disaster that appears to confront us in the fact of the population explosion of our time. H. G. Wells, the prophet and protagonist of the scientific world-view, left as his last will and testament a book with the title 'Mind at the end of its tether'. Because our minds are so acutely aware of the sheer magnitude of the forces operating in the world we easily surrender to the sense of futility. 'Nothing I can do can make any difference.'

We must take this widely prevalent mood of twentieth-century man seriously and not try to evade its disconcerting challenge by pointing to the indisputable fact that there are still large numbers of men in the twentieth century for whom God is beyond question the most self-luminous of realities, the only hypothesis which even begins to make sense. The fact that these 'large numbers' are nevertheless a minority need not dismay us. After all a true understanding of God has always been a minority opinion. But for our understanding of the evangelistic task of our generation it is of the first importance that we take seriously two facts—the prevailing opinion *and* the subtly penetrating power of the prevailing opinion to erode the confidence of the minority which believes. False ideas of God can be corrected. It is much more difficult to correct no idea of God. That is the dilemma we confront as we meet Western man, and as to an increasing extent in Asia and Africa we face 'Westernized man', the man who, to quote Toynbee, has taken the husk of Western civilization and rejected its kernel.

Let us analyse the situation a little further. During the first World War Rudyard Kipling wrote a somewhat mordant and bitter poem in six stanzas with the general title 'Natural Theology'.

In the first stanza a primitive man speaks:

> I ate my fill of a whale that died
>   And stranded after a month at sea. . . .
> There is a pain in my inside.
>   Why have the Gods afflicted me?

> Ow! I am purged till I am a wraith!
>> Wow! I am sick till I cannot see!
> What is the sense of religion and faith?
>> Look how the Gods have afflicted me!

Then a pagan speaks:

> How can the skin of a rat or mouse hold
>> Anything more than a harmless flea?
> The burning plague has taken my household.
>> Why have my Gods afflicted me?
> All my kith and kin are deceased,
>> Though they were as good as good could be,
> I will out and batter the family priest,
>> Because my Gods have afflicted me!

A mediaeval man takes up the tale:

> My privy and well drain into each other
>> After the custom of Christendie. . . .
> Fevers and fluxes are wasting my mother.
>> Why has the Lord afflicted me?
> The saints are helpless for all I offer—
>> So are the clergy I used to fee.
> Henceforward I keep my cash in my coffer,
>> Because the Lord has afflicted me!

The voice of a late nineteenth-century man is then heard:

> I run eight hundred hens to the acre
>> They die by dozens mysteriously. . . .
> I am more than doubtful concerning my Maker.
>> Why has the Lord afflicted me?
> What a return for all my endeavour—
>> Not to mention the L.S.D.!
> I am an atheist now and for ever
>> Because this God has afflicted me!

This is followed by a figure we can recognize as our contemporary—the man who has lived through two world
wars and faces the prospect of a third, who has seen the
moral fabric of society begin to disintegrate. He speaks:

> Money spent on an Army or Fleet
>> Is homicidal lunacy. . . .
> My son has been killed in the Mons retreat.
>> Why is the Lord afflicting me?
> Why are murder, pillage and arson
>> And rape allowed by the Deity?
> I will write to *The Times*, deriding our parson
>> Because my God has afflicted me!

Kipling then makes the five of them speak in chorus linking the sublime and the trivial:

> We had a kettle: we let it leak:
>> Our not repairing it made it worse.
> We haven't had any tea for a week. . . .
>> The bottom is out of the universe.

Before we take note of Kipling's closing verse it is important for our analysis to recognize that, however caricatured, the poem does give us a fair picture of natural theology, that is the theology of the natural man. And it is a genuine theology, it is a word or explanation about God. However erroneous the fundamental attitude to God might be, there was a fundamental attitude to God. He was a God who could be misunderstood, resented and rejected, but he was there.

Kipling's last verse is in a curious way an anticipation of our contemporary scene in our 'do it yourself world'. The last verse runs:

> This was none of the good Lord's pleasure,
>> For the Spirit he breathed in man is free;
> But what comes after is measure for measure,
>> And not a God that afflicteth thee.
> As was the sowing so the reaping
>> Is now and evermore shall be.
> Thou art delivered to thine own keeping
>> Only Thyself hath afflicted thee!

The cadences and even the theology of that last verse are profoundly true to *one* searching element in the Biblical

message. We do well to remember Romans, ch. 1, vv. 21-24:
'. . . all their thinking has ended in futility. . . . God has
given them up'; and Ephesians, ch. 2, v. 12: '. . . a world
without hope and without God'. To be 'delivered to thine
own keeping' is to know in a new way what it is to be
'isolated, alone and afraid'. There would seem to be at least
some contemporary evidence that many today are beginning
to feel that there is a degree of isolation and aloneness, with
constant fear, which is strictly speaking intolerable—something which cannot be borne.

There is a suggestive little point in the last line of
Kipling's poem when it is seen in print—'Only Thyself hath
afflicted thee'. Thyself has a capital 'T'. God has been
argued out of existence. In that case I really am 'on my
own'. In a terribly individual sense, then, each one of us
must echo the word, so often recorded in the prophecy of
Isaiah, 'I am God and there is none else: there is no God
beside *me*.'

But the concluding verse of Kipling's poem, true though
it is to one of the sombre threads which runs through Scripture, does not, thank God, give us the whole truth.

There is a sermon by one B. D. Napier, the source of
which I cannot trace, which contains a suggestive alternative version of Isaiah, ch. 6, which runs like this:

> In the year that King Uzziah died, I resolved that with
> the help of God I would think only positive thoughts and so
> come to believe in myself. And suddenly I saw myself sitting
> on a throne high and lifted up: and I knew my own strength
> and power, and I said 'I will stamp on my mind a mental
> picture of myself as succeeding', and when I said 'Who will
> help me?', the Lord said, 'Here am I, use Me'.

The humility of God and his infinite patience is the other
strand in Scripture which matches and more than matches
man's consistent misunderstandings of God.

Before, however, we are ready to explore this more
hopeful prospect, there is one very important aspect of the
contemporary sense of futility which we must take into

consideration. This can perhaps be described as a loss of faith in history, a fundamental scepticism about there being any purpose, any direction whatever in human affairs. We see this in the paradox of a world which is demonstrably an economically interdependent world, a world in which technical skills have developed so far that all the basic material needs of men could be met without serious difficulty; and yet this same world is characterized by each nation furiously insisting on its own independence while its technological skills are devoted to trying to bolster an independence which is technologically absurd.

At the very moment when the processes of all past history have made it at last possible for all men to enter into the enjoyment of one common universal history, a veritable 'City of God' into which each nation would bring its treasures, our human perversity compels us to echo the words of Hezekiah:

> This day is a day of distress, of rebuke, and of disgrace; children have come to the birth, and there is no strength to bring them forth. (II Kings 19.3; Isa. 37.3, RSV)

Such is the underlying reality of our world in its contemporary futility, a futility which is leading to increasing despair, and with despair a spirit of anarchic violence, which is an ominous phenomenon in country after country. If we are shut up to futility, if history is without meaning, without purpose, without direction, then 'every man for himself and the devil take the hindmost'.

This is the situation in which the Christian has to bear his witness to the fact that history has got a meaning, and to affirm what that meaning is. And he has to do this whether the world listens or does not listen. It cannot be too strongly insisted that while Christians are under an obligation to present the truth in a way that men can understand, they are not given any assurance that their presentation will be accepted. A reasonable faith, a related religion and a relevant Church may all be rejected. Rejection does not mean that the faith was unreasonable, the religion unrelated to life, the Church irrelevant. That said, there remains the Christian obligation—the obligation, as someone has recently expressed it, not so much to find new ideas and new words to express old truths,

> but rather new forms of obedience, new structures of life which express for our time and place the relation to God— the participation in his history—which the biblical story inspires. The reality which the Christian confesses is not a claim for a given set of ideas or for a given institution. Rather by this reality theology is turned into a secular discipline and the Church into a secular institution, each having its relevance to a time and place, each being true only in the sense that it is a faithful reflection of the action of God there and then.[1]

In that quotation there is an important clause which demands close attention. The writer, once a missionary in China and with an extensive knowledge of Christians behind the iron curtain, is not using the word 'secular' as meaning the opposite of sacred. Rather he would wish us to understand by 'secular' that which belongs properly to this present age in the purpose of God, this precise world of our own time which is itself sacred, sanctified as it is by the presence of God active in it. The antithesis between sacred and secular is and always has been an essentially false antithesis. The very heart of the Biblical revelation lies in 'the Word made flesh', in the sacred secularity of an event at a particular moment in history which gives meaning to all history.

Our Christian obligation then is to discover what this must mean for our day. And the quotation given just now presents us with the essential nature of our task. We are to find 'new forms of obedience, new structures of life' by which we can express for our time and place the relation of the world to God.

[1] Charles C. West, 'The Obsolescence of History', *The Ecumenical Review*, Jan. 1965, Vol. XVII, No. 1.

This involves for us the necessity to take this world and every aspect of life in our world with real seriousness.

> Teach me, my God and King,
>   In all things Thee to see;
> And what I do in anything
>   To do it as for Thee.

So sang George Herbert, and so we often sing forgetting perhaps that these words must be held to cover much that appears trivial and of little importance.

> All may of Thee partake;
>   Nothing can be so mean
> Which, with this tincture, 'for thy sake',
>   Will not grow bright and clean.

This is the basic attitude to life, to all of this world in its very secularity, which we must learn to acquire if we are to serve this present age and God within it.

But immediately we become humble enough not to 'despise the day of small things' we discover that in fact we have adopted a certain attitude to history. For if God comes in the little things then *a fortiori* he is to be discovered at work in 'the high tumultuous lists of life'. Seeing upon what small fidelities in life great issues turn we must believe that God is concerned with these great issues. He who could bid a prophet find meaning in a bud of almond blossom, and a common kitchen cooking pot, also bade the prophet relate what he saw to the international political scene, the march of armies and the struggle of empires.

Let us be clear that this involves for us a tremendous act of faith. Perhaps the most dramatic illustration of such a faith is to be found in the perplexity of the prophet Habakkuk as he looked out upon the world of his time. A brutal and utterly callous imperial power was threatening the peace of the world and the prospects of his own nation's survival. Having a strong sense of God's providential ordering of history, he expostulates with God both about the chaos of the total world situation and the moral and spiritual confusion in his own country. But, note, he expostulates with God. He trusts God in the deepest dimensions of faith. And God then leads him out into a new understanding of history. It was surely one of the greatest moments in the long story of religion when to that prophet's consciousness came the staggeringly unexpected revelation which accompanied the words:

> Look among the nations, and see;
> wonder and be astounded.
> For I am doing a work in your days
> that you would not believe if told.
> For lo, I am rousing the Chaldeans,
> that bitter and hasty nation,
> who march through the breadth of the earth,
> to seize habitations not their own.
>
> (Hab. 1. 5-6, RSV)

What a major challenge to faith that must have been, that discovery that the God of the covenant people of Israel accepted personal responsibility for the actions of a hostile power which threatened their very existence! The discovery came just in time. Only a few years later the covenant people were in fact overrun by that very power and their leaders taken into exile.

We will surely not be very far off the mark if we attribute something of the incredible persistence of the Jewish people, their survival as a self-conscious community to the reactions of the prophet Habakkuk to this unexpected interpretation of international politics, a reaction which was a distinctive and unique characteristic of the great prophets of Israel. Habakkuk said:

> I will take my stand to watch,
> and station myself on the tower,
> and look forth to see what he will say to me,
> and what I will answer concerning my complaint.
>
> (Hab. 2.1, RSV)

Here is faith operating as a hypothesis and being submitted to the test of experience. And Habakkuk hears God's answer:

> Write the vision;
> make it plain upon tablets,
> so he may run who reads it (Hab 2.2, RSV)

—recording history. That is what is involved in writing the vision. But patient experimentation remains the test of scientist and believer:

> For still the vision awaits its time;
> it hastens to the end—it will not lie.
> If it seem slow, wait for it;
>   it will surely come, it will not delay. (Hab. 2.3, RSV)

It is no accident that centuries later St Paul took the next verse as the basis for his doctrine of justification by grace through faith:

> Behold, he whose soul is not upright in him shall fail,
> but the righteous shall live by his faith. (Hab. 2.4, RSV)

In the prophet the word 'faith' signifies faithfulness, in the sense of fidelity. But the link between that and St Paul's faith-obedience is direct and immediate. But for our purpose it is valuable to lay the accent at this point upon 'fidelity'. For it takes no great leap of imagination to translate this into 'new forms of obedience, new structures of life'. Historically, that is precisely what in fact happened to the people of Israel. Their history is a fascinating record of continual adjustment to 'new forms of obedience, new structures of life'. Here is one clue to understanding the Bible. A nomadic people becomes a settled agricultural community: a central tent of meeting yields to innumerable local shrines: these in turn are found to be inadequate and a central temple is erected: but cultus however magnificent can become unrelated to social needs and the prophet has to balance the priest: then comes exile in a strange land where it is difficult to sing the Lord's song, where processions and sacrifice are not possible: and so synagogue worship is developed: religion becomes individual as well as corporate. Such is the pattern of history as Israel discovered it. Interestingly enough a similar pattern can be discovered in the missionary outreach of the new Israel.

Such is the way in which the Bible takes history seriously, and links the great movements of political, economic and social life to the experience of the individual, giving to the individual at once a dignity of his own which makes him meaningful as a person, and at the same time a sense of proportion which conduces to humility, for he is the servant of the God who reveals himself as being the maker and the servant of history.

If, then, we take the Bible as our guide to history, that is, the sphere in which we discover God and man—for that discovery is what gives to history its coherence—we can claim that there we discover the humility, the patience and the forgiveness of God, a humility, a patience and a forgiveness which characterizes all his relationship with nations and persons, with man in his various collectivities and man in his individuality.

The question we have to ask ourselves is, 'Do we believe this?' And that means a great deal more than an intellectual assent to a proposition. It means what Habakkuk meant by faith: it means a 'form of obedience', 'a structure of life'. And this means for each of us an individual discipline.

I have never forgotten a lesson I learnt many years ago from a friend of mine who was an outstandingly brilliant conjurer. Once, fascinated by a display of virtuosity in which he appeared to be handling six different balls with consummate ease, and apparently without any attention, for all the while he was entertaining us with patter, I asked him how much practice this particular act involved. To my astonishment he said that that particular act had taken him five hours' practice every day for two years. What I was watching was a superb demonstration of freedom, behind which lay hours and hours of disciplined drudgery, of exhausting physical endurance, of infinite patience and perseverance.

We may assume that all great artists would have the same story to tell. Is it to be expected that the art of living will be any different, or the art of being a minister, a servant? For that is our calling, both as individuals and as members of the servant community which is the Church.

In the prophecy of Isaiah there came those passages which are known as the 'Servant Songs'. It is well known to students that it is not easy to distinguish between the servant as a community and the servant as an individual. And even of the Servant in Isaiah, ch. 53, we may well ask with the Ethiopian eunuch:

> Tell me, please, who it is that the prophet is speaking about here: himself or someone else? (Acts 8.34)

With the missionary, Philip, we are bold to start from this passage and tell 'the good news of Jesus'. That, however, remains for us as it was for Philip an act of faith. No doubt already, in that very young Christian community, hints dropped by our Lord had been meditated upon by his disciples, and so already Isaiah 53 was read as an anticipation of the Messiah, an interpretation, by the way, which had never been given to it by any Jewish teacher before. What was it that so completely convinced the early Christian Church; what is it that makes us endorse this interpretation; who but the Christ of Calvary? At the Cross words became action, something spoken and written became something done. A flood of illumination was suddenly thrown upon history. All the humility, patience and forgiveness of God which the prophet had described in that matchless picture, had now been matched before men's eyes.

What had always been at the heart of God, what had been glimpsed by prophetic souls, was now placarded before the eyes of men, offering to them, if they would, a clue to the meaning of history, a way of understanding its frustrations and futilities, seeing these as reflections of what William James once described as:

> something wild in the universe which we with all our idealities and faithfulnesses are needed to redeem; and first of all to redeem our own hearts from atheisms and fears.[1]

There is a link there with the prophet Habakkuk. But we know that it takes more to redeem our souls than enlisting our own 'idealities and faithfulnesses'. The atheisms and fears which paralyse us into thinking all effort is futile, which lead us to barren anger in moments of frustration, all that makes us slaves to the spirit of the age, these need a power of redemption outside ourselves.

Once allow Christ and him crucified to be indeed the express image of the invisible God: once see him as 'the richness of God's free grace lavished upon us, imparting full wisdom and insight' (Eph. 1.7-8), and we begin to see history, all mankind and ourselves in a new way. We discover 'the hidden purpose of God' (Eph. 1.9). The Cross is the beginning of the end of futility and it is that for two reasons. As the Bible presents it the Cross has a cosmic significance, transcending as well as including history. And it also speaks to me as an individual. 'The Son of God . . . loved me and sacrificed himself for me.' There can be no futility if 'my present bodily life is lived by faith in the Son of God' (Gal. 2.20).

'Therefore, my beloved brothers, stand firm and immovable, and work for the Lord always, work without limit, since you know that in the Lord, your labour cannot be lost' (I Cor. 15.58).

[1] William James, *The Will to Believe*, pp. 61-2.

4

The Cross and our Fear
of Death

RUDOLF BULTMANN, in his study of the meaning of the words 'Life' and 'Death', as we find them used in the Bible, has this to say by way of summing up the significance of what the New Testament records:

> The prevailing idea is that, in Christ, God was dealing with the world (II Cor. 5.19) and that in such action by God Christ was taking death upon himself and thus death has lost its destructive character and taken on the creative character of divine action. Thus in his death resurrection is established. This act of dying has finished with sin and thus with death; out of it grew life.[1]

Let us begin where we are and consider how men feel about death today. Is there anything in the modern world which corresponds with what the writer of the Letter to the Hebrews describes as the condition of those who 'through fear of death were all their lifetime subject to bondage' (Heb. 2.15, AV)? Those are strong words. We can readily acknowledge that classical writers were burdened with the fear of death or, at least, with hopelessness in the face of its inevitability. Death made a mockery of life. Superb expression is given to the mood of that old world in a passage in Robert Browning's poem 'Cleon' which deserves quoting at some length. Cleon, a poet, is writing to a friend in reply to a letter in which that friend has urged the poet not to

[1] Rudolf Bultmann *et al.*, *Life and Death* (Adam and Charles Black, London 1965), p. 94.

distress himself with death but satisfy himself that in his poems he will be immortal. This thought gives Cleon no pleasure at all. And the poem at this point reads on:

> my fate is deadlier still,
> In this, that every day my sense of joy
> Grows more acute, my soul (intensified
> By power and insight) more enlarged, more keen;
> While every day my hairs fall more and more,
> My hand shakes, and the heavy years increase—
> The horror quickening still from year to year,
> The consummation coming past escape
> When I shall know most, and yet least enjoy—
> When all my works wherein I prove my worth,
> Being present still to mock me in men's mouths,
> Alive still, in the praise of such as thou,
> I, I the feeling, thinking, acting man,
> The man who loved his life so over-much,
> Sleep in my urn. It is so horrible,
> I dare at times imagine to my need
> Some future state revealed to us by Zeus,
> Unlimited in capability
> For Joy, as this is in desire for Joy,
> —To seek which, the joy-hunger forces us:
> That, stung by straitness of our life, made strait
> On purpose to make prized the life at large—
> Freed by the throbbing impulse we call death,
> We burst there as the worm into the fly,
> Who, while a worm still, wants his wings.
>   But no!
> Zeus has not yet revealed it; and alas,
> He must have done so, were it possible!

There, with great fidelity, Browning expresses the mood of the ancient world into which Paul and his companions came preaching 'Jesus and the Resurrection'. How passionately, how hopelessly, men then longed for

> Some future state. . . .
> Unlimited in capability
> For joy, as this is in desire for joy.

To quote Bultmann again:

> Although in the old popular Greek view death does not mean a complete end of human existence, in so far as the dead man leads a shadowy existence in Hades, this does not really count as life. What life really means is ended by death and no one must underrate the horror of death. Life is the highest good . . . the inevitability of death casts its shadow over every life and puts a question-mark against its whole meaning.[1]

Perhaps we react differently, but can we say that the difference is really fundamental? Anyone who has read Evelyn Waugh's satirical novel, *The Loved One*, will have caught a glimpse into the modern attempt to escape from the horror of death by pretending there is nothing horrible about it. That book describes the activity of a mortician's paradise in Los Angeles where a vast business is built up in the attempt to disguise the meaning of our mortality. Bodies are embalmed, re-created in a revolting pretence that they are alive, and farewell parties are arranged for the mourners to come and see 'the loved one' as he or she is not in death and almost certainly never was in life. The book is a horror-comic, because it shows the attempt to avoid the stark realism of the grave.

This elaborate make-believe is sure evidence of a refusal to come to terms with death. It is the fear of death repressed, driven below the level of consciousness, ready when least expected to reveal itself. To quote Robert Browning again:

> Just when we are safest, there's a sunset-touch,
> A fancy from a flower-bell, some one's death,
> A chorus-ending from Euripides,—
> And that's enough for fifty hopes and fears
> As old and new at once as nature's self,
> To rap and knock and enter in our soul,
> Take hands and dance there, a fantastic ring,
> Round the ancient idol, on his base again,—
> The grand Perhaps![2]

[1] Rudolf Bultmann, op. cit., pp. 27-8.
[2] Robert Browning, 'Bishop Blougram's Apology'.

There is still another attitude, and one very common today, to which Somerset Maugham has given expression in his book *The Summing Up*. He writes:

> If then one puts aside the existence of God and the possibility of survival as too doubtful to have any effect on one's behaviour, one has to make up one's mind what is the meaning and use of life. If death ends all, if I have neither to hope for good to come nor to fear evil, I must ask myself what I am here for, and how in these circumstances I must conduct myself.
>
> Now [he goes on] the answer to one of these questions is plain, but it is so unpalatable that most men will not face it. There is no reason for life, and life has no meaning.[1]

Death ends all, so an increasing number of people appear to believe. If so, then Maugham is surely right and life has no meaning for it lacks any dimension of depth. Our apparent experiences of depth, those intimations of immortality which come in our sudden awareness of beauty, our discoveries of truth, our sense of rightness and wrongness, our capacity for love, these are illusory, or at least ephemeral. They point to nothing beyond themselves. Let us eat, drink and copulate, for tomorrow we die. It almost looks as if we are going to be driven to admitting that without the fear of death we cannot fully enjoy life! Were the medievals then right in working out their elaborate geography of death, for ever enshrined in the magic of Dante's great construction? No doubt they pressed their logic too far. But in a Europe racked by plague, pestilence and famine, by battle, murder and sudden death, they did preserve the fundamental Christian conviction that death was not the end of life. They practised the conviction that as life is a preparation for death, so death is a preparation for life. It matters how you live because that will determine how you die. So how you die will bear upon the life after death.

[1] Somerset Maugham, *The Summing Up* (William Heinemann, Collected Edition 1948), pp. 271-2.

Consider our contemporary world. For many people life is accepted in Somerset Maugham's terms, as being meaningless because death is the end, the negation of life's meaning. One sequel is an appalling lack of respect for life—for human beings as living persons. And I am not just thinking of the sheer brutality with which men treat each other. Man's inhumanity to man is no new thing. But even in this respect the callous carelessness of human life in earlier ages is being replaced by a more calculating brutality today. Far more serious, however, is the ability men have acquired with which to assault the inner citadel of the personality, and to deface a person by brain-washing. The most formidable description of what this can mean of which I know is to be found in the first chapter of Charles Morgan's *Liberties of the Mind*. I commend it as demonstrating the truth of a sentence there recorded which closed a conversation between an American scientist and Charles Morgan. They had been discussing the increasing ability of modern science to recondition men's minds involuntarily. Charles Morgan had challenged the moral validity of such action. This had surprised the American, who used the familiar argument about not being able to stop progress. Nevertheless, he was somewhat shaken in his assurance. In parting he remarked:

It all depends, doesn't it, not so much on what one thinks that men can do as on what one believes a man is?[1]

Precisely! What does one believe a man is? Are we but

such stuff
As dreams are made on, and our little life
Is rounded with a sleep,[2]

or do we sleep to wake, die to live? If indeed we die to live, then a preparation for death will be an essential way of looking at life; and a fear of death will be an indispensable

[1] Charles Morgan, *Liberties of the Mind* (Macmillan, London 1951). See Chapter I, 'Introduction: Mind Control', p. 16.
[2] William Shakespeare, *The Tempest*, Act 4, sc. 1.

element in respect for life, in ourselves and other people. For great issues turn on death.

What has Scripture to say about death? The prevailing Old Testament conviction is a conviction about life. Yahveh is the God of life. He is the life-giver and the life-preserver. Death in the Old Testament is seen, for the most part, as breaking the relationship between man and Yahveh. 'The dead praise not Yahveh', say the Psalmists (Pss. 6.5; 30.9; 88.5, 10). The most poignant utterance of all on this theme is found in the words of Hezekiah, after his recovery from sickness, as recorded in Isaiah. After giving vivid expression to his views of death, Hezekiah, grateful for having his life spared for a few more years, exults 'the living, the living, he thanks thee, as I do this day' (Isa. 38.9-18, RSV).

Now it is interesting to note that this pessimism about death does not lead the man of the Old Testament to take Somerset Maugham's attitude to life. Life for the man of the Old Testament is the time and opportunity for knowing God. This is the conviction which gives meaning to life; and it was this conviction which slowly but surely changed the attitude of Old Testament man towards death.

This God of life was a God who did business with men. He called them by name, and he made covenants with them. Most decisive of all was the covenant made in the wilderness where a rabble of refugees was fused into a people for whom, corporately, life, that is history, began to make sense. It is not easy or even possible to get a clear picture of what that decisive experience was, but it shaped all subsequent history. What is more, it became the norm by which this particular people judged themselves. In the first place they became aware, and the awareness grew with the centuries, that there was a continuity about God which was not affected by the apparent discontinuity of man. And this continuity of God found expression in the continuity of Israel, as a people upon whom God had laid his hand. This in turn posed for men the question of God's justice. If God was God, and was indeed a just and holy God, then he must surely distinguish between those who sought to obey him and those who refused to obey him. Yet death came to all alike. There was no easy answer to this fact of one end common to the good man and the bad man, to the wise man and the fool.

The preacher in Ecclesiastes makes the point as bitingly as Somerset Maugham:

> One event happeneth to them all. Then said I in my heart, As it happeneth to the fool, so it happeneth even to me; and why was I then more wise? Then I said in my heart, that this also is vanity. For there is no remembrance of the wise more than of the fool for ever. . . . And how dieth the wise man? as the fool. Therefore I hated life; because the work that is wrought under the sun is grievous unto me: for all is vanity and vexation of spirit. (Eccles. 2.14-17, AV)

That is one point of view, a point of view which took death seriously but without hope, and came very near to denying life. But there is also in the Old Testament another voice. It is the voice of those who consistently gave the highest value to life, and found its meaning in obedience to what they were discovering about the nature and will of the God they worshipped. For over the centuries the holiness of God became more and more obviously a characteristic which had to be reflected by the man who worshipped God. The idea of the holy became moralized. From taking life thus seriously some men, at least, found it quite impossible to believe that a relationship thus entered into by the individual with God could be any less continuous than was the life of the whole people with the same God—the God of the Covenants.

This other view is expressed in Isaiah:

> Thy dead shall live, their bodies shall rise.
> O dwellers in the dust, awake and sing for joy!
> For thy dew is a dew of light,
> and on the land of the shades thou wilt let it fall.
> (Isa. 26.19, RSV)

That is a magnificent burgeoning of faith in the grace of God, a grace still of limited reference to Israel, as an earlier verse (v. 14) makes clear, but grace nevertheless, a miracle unearned by man but wholly consistent with God's own character. And because God is so good to Israel he can be trusted to be as good to the individual Israelite. This is the burden of the closing verses of Psalm 73.

> I am continually with thee: thou hast holden me by my right hand. Thou shalt guide me with thy counsel, and afterward receive me to glory. Whom have I in heaven but thee? and there is none upon earth that I desire beside thee. My flesh and my heart faileth: but God is the strength of my heart, and my portion for ever. (Ps. 73.23-26, AV)

Life, in a word, is more powerful than death.

I have dwelt thus long on the Old Testament to bring out the fact of great significance that the meaning of life is fellowship with God, that this is its dimension of depth. Once that meaning is accepted, then, sooner or later, death for all its apparent finality, is seen to have at its heart a mystery. God is not bound by death for God is life. How then is it possible to conclude that those who have found life to be life with God can ever lose what they have found? This is not a proof about life after death. But it does suggest that a certain way of life is the best preparation for dying, while hope is fixed upon the God who has been known in life.

The Old Testament is a book about life. But it is not simply a book about the present life. It is open-ended. It looks increasingly to the future, a future which God will inaugurate, the same God revealed in the past and the present. It is, therefore, a book best understood as a book full of hope, not least hope about the future of the people of God, and about the individual who is one of this people.

Now the New Testament is a book about the life after death. That is the key to its understanding. The New Testament does not discount the Old Testament, least of all in its emphasis upon life. But it completes it by fulfilling its hope.

The very heart of the New Testament is the message of Easter, that he who was dead is alive.

But this being alive from the dead must not be divorced from the death itself. It was precisely because the Man had actually died, died as completely as any man can die, that the fact that he did not remain dead is so fundamentally important. Professor Moule of Cambridge has put it forcibly like this:

> Here was a man, ready to go to any lengths in the service of others—affirming by his life, and then by his death, that love was to him ultimately important; and doing so in the name of God. And when the point of no return had been reached—he did return. This is the extraordinary conviction that overtook and forced itself upon the men and women who had known him best and for whom his death had done its worst.[1]

Why is the death so important? The answer is to be found in mankind's universal experience of death. If Jesus did not die on the Cross, as Muslims, for instance, insist, then he did not 'rise from the dead'. In that case what the disciples experienced later was no more than the conviction that they had lived in fellowship with a remarkable personality—if you like it, the most remarkable personality who had ever lived. Like some of their predecessors, of whom they read in their Scriptures, they might well feel that they had had an experience of God in the person of Jesus. But in what conceivable sense could they be set free from the fear of death (to quote Heb. 2.15), as they undoubtedly were, unless they were completely convinced that 'the last enemy' had, in fact, been destroyed? Now all the writers of the New Testament may have been mistaken, and all who have believed what they believed ever since may have lived by the same mistake. That must be taken seriously as a possibility.

---

[1] See *Faith, Fact and Fantasy* by four authors, including a chapter by C. F. D. Moule, *Is Christ Unique?* (Fontana Books, Collins 1964), pp. 116-17.

But there is much more at stake in the reality of Christ's death on the Cross. For that dying was a judgment passed by men upon themselves. On the Cross we see in its starkest understanding these words in St John's Gospel:

This is the judgment, *the crisis of mankind*, that the light is come into the world, and men loved the darkness rather than the light; for their works were evil (John 3.19, RV),

or, as the New English Bible translates it:

Here lies the test: the light has come into the world, but men preferred darkness to light because their deeds were evil.

'Christ on the Cross'—that is man hating the highest when he sees it and crucifying it—that is the judgment on humanity in so far as humanity is willing to remain identified with sin. That is what man, left to himself, does with goodness, and the end of that doing is death. Man has not only to be rescued from death; he has to be rescued from the doing which leads to death. Only so can the fear of death be lifted, the fear of its finality, of its ultimate denial of any meaning to life.

What the men who wrote the New Testament books, after living out the New Testament experience, had proved for themselves was that by the death on the Cross they had been revealed to themselves as what they really were, and had discovered that, nevertheless, God loved them. And they made this tremendous leap of imagination, or if you will, of faith, and insisted that in a way past understanding God was all the while loving them from the Cross.

Sin could not stop God loving. The tragic link between sin and death was broken on the Cross. And this was altogether an act of God. Life then, as freedom from the power of sin and the fear of death, follows upon what Bultmann would insist is 'adhering in faith to an historical fact and an historical person'.[1] Our argument must carry us a little further. For we must understand what it means to 'adhere in faith'

[1] Rudolf Bultmann, op. cit., p. 76.

to this historical fact, this historical person. We can only test the truth that in Christ God was dealing with the world (as our opening quotation had it) if we know in experience that he is dealing with our world, and in particular with that individual bit of our world which for each of us is our real world.

There is a word of Jesus recorded by St Luke which deals very specifically indeed with our own little individual worlds, the worlds of our own distinctive relationships. He says: 'Whoever does not bear his own cross, and come after me, cannot be my disciple' (Luke 14.27, RSV). The whole context of these words is profoundly challenging and the passage ends: 'So likewise, whosoever he be of you that forsaketh not all that he hath, he cannot be my disciple' (Luke 14.33, AV). In St Mark's Gospel there is a slightly different wording and the context is a quite different one. But the demand is the same:

> If any man would come after me, let him deny himself, and take up his cross, and follow me. For whosoever would save his life shall lose it; and whosoever shall lose his life for my sake and the Gospel's shall save it. (Mark 8.34-35, RV)

These passages point to something quite fundamental to our triumph over the fear of death, something quite indispensable to our preparation for death. Assuming that we wish to follow Christ, that is that our believing in him, 'adhering in faith to his historical person', carries with it identification with him on the Cross: assuming that we have accepted the Cross as a true verdict on ourselves, and as a true revelation of the nature of God: assuming all this, then life must be for us, as it was for Jesus, a continual saying 'no' to self-will, to all that wills selfishly. This means in practice a daily dying—a letting go—a losing of life for the sake of Christ and his Gospel. Nor will we find it easy. Just as our physical nature rebels against its dissolution, so our minds and spirits hate the death of self-will. We too have to learn day by day what it means to set the face steadfastly on the way up to Jerusalem. But it is the testimony of nearly twenty centuries of Christian experience that in this way, and only in this way, do we discover the meaning of Christ's Cross and its immediate relevance for holy living and holy dying.

'For the sake of Christ and his Gospel' is a reference full of meaning. As we adhere by faith to this historical person we are caught up in the historical fact that he is not just a figure in the past. He is the head of his Church in the present. St John can say:

> We for our part have crossed over from death to life; this we know, because we love our brothers. The one who does not love is still in the realm of death. (I John 3.14)

And the same Epistle reminds us that the Gospel is

> the remedy for the defilement of our sins, not our sins only but the sins of all the world. (I John 2.2)

Because we are in Christ, in Christ crucified and risen, we know that we are part of something cosmic in its range because death has lost its destructive character and taken on the creative character of divine action.

We now are part of that divine action. 'Thus in his death', which we share, 'resurrection is established'. 'This act of dying', in which again we share, 'has finished with sin and thus with death'.

Out of all this grows life.

5

The Cross in our Ministry
of Healing

HEALTH, WHOLENESS, integrity, holiness—these
words express different shades of meaning of the same
reality which lies at the root of all existence, of human
existence and of the whole created order. Else it would not
be possible for the primal verdict on creation to have been
that 'God saw everything that he had made, and, behold it
was very good' (Gen. 1.31, AV).

This affirmative attitude towards creation, this saying 'yes'
to life, is the radically Biblical view of the whole created
order. Nature, as we observe it, no doubt gives ample
evidence of anarchic forces, is all too often experienced as
'red in tooth and claw'. Human kind has defaced the divine
image to a point where it is easy to despair. Man's inhumanity to man gives a nightmare quality to life. Yet our
affirmation stands if we accept the Biblical interpretation of
existence and experience. Either the basis of human life and
society, as of the natural order, is health, wholeness, integrity and holiness, or we have two choices—a purposeless
universe on the one hand, or a rejection of the material
world as a prison house from which the only purpose of man
is to escape. One view denies God altogether. The other
takes a pessimistic view of his intelligence for ever having
made the world at all. Both, in effect, are world-denying.
Biblical faith is world-affirming.

But in being world-affirming Biblical faith is not looking
at things through rose-coloured spectacles. It sees the created
order groaning in all its parts 'as if in the pangs of child-

birth' (Rom. 8.22), and it likewise sees the human race 'groaning inwardly while we wait for God to make us his sons and set our whole body free' (Rom. 8.23).

In that dramatic passage in Romans, ch. 8, the Apostle, who in that same Letter has given such a devastating picture of the power of evil in human life, stakes everything on the fact that the first word and the last word about man and his world is goodness, because the first and the last word belong to God.

If we are to exercise a ministry of healing in a world which is manifestly sick, out of sorts in an infinite variety of ways, it will make all the difference to our ministry if we are convinced that we are working 'with' the grain of the universe and not 'against' it. If, like the medical practitioner, we can be assured that in every human situation there is a *vis mediatrix naturae* upon which we can rely as part of the constitution of the sick person or the sick society, we can approach every individual and every situation, even the most intractable, with hope. This is the practical effect of a belief in God.

The healing power of nature, an observable fact in the physical realm, translated into terms of our common humanity can be described as the ground of our being, or in Pauline language 'Christ in you—hope' (Col. 1.27). For realists that hope is 'hope of a glory to come'. It looks towards a realization throughout our whole human nature, as throughout the created world, of a harmony which has always been the divine intention. We may say, indeed, using contemporary language, that this divine intention has been 'built in' to man, and to the universe. That intention has been frustrated. It has not been defeated. So it is that in the same chapter of Colossians, St Paul can say

Formerly you were yourselves estranged from God; you were his enemies in heart and mind, and your deeds were evil. But now by Christ's death in his body of flesh and blood God has reconciled you to himself, so that he may present you before himself as dedicated men, without blemish and innocent in his sight. Only you must continue in your faith, firm on your foundations, never to be dislodged from the hope offered in the gospel which you heard. This is the gospel which has been proclaimed in the whole creation under heaven; and I, Paul, have become its minister. (Col. 1.21-23)

If we take that passage seriously, and if necessary translate it further into more contemporary thought forms, we find in it the foundation conviction that the Cross is a tremendous affirmation. Christ on his Cross is not simply denying the power of evil, he is positively asserting the power of good. He is revealing that in the worst circumstances there is a healing power at work.

The ministry of healing draws its power from an un-quenchable certainty about the fundamental character of health. And this unquenchable certainty derives from the fact that Christ plumbed the depths of human nature, ex-periencing its temptations and its weakness, its frustrations and its despair, and never losing faith in it because in the very ground of man's being he found God. The conversation of the Cross was neither a monologue nor a dialogue but a conversation piece within the very heart of God and of Man.

The Cross on Calvary, Christ upon that Cross, speaks more directly into the human situation, into the dilemmas of society and the distress of the individual, than any other revelation, than any other intimation of the nature of reality. Men may misunderstand the Cross and reject what they mis-understand. They may find it impossible to accept because of its implications. They may rate it as too wonderful to be credible. But it has their vote to prove itself true if it can. It does draw all men. It haunts all men. And it does all this because it is a beacon of hope, quite irrespective of anything that theologians may make of it. It is a 'yes' flung in the face of all the negations of life.

Some years ago on one Good Friday, I was unable, through circumstances, to join any fellow Christians in a corporate meditation at the Cross. Instead, I spent a large part of the day quietly at home using the opportunity to try to understand a little more fully something of the healing power of our Lord as he hung upon the Cross.

My own thinking that day began with a study of the Collects specially appointed for Good Friday in the Book of Common Prayer. One word which had never struck me before arrested my attention. The first of the Collects for Good Friday reads as follows:

> Almighty God, we beseech thee graciously to behold this thy family, for which our Lord Jesus Christ was *contented* to be betrayed, and given up into the hands of wicked men, and to suffer death upon the cross, who now liveth and reigneth with thee and the Holy Ghost, ever one God, world without end.

The word in that Collect which came to me with an entirely new force was the word 'contented'. And it came with the force of a challenge. For that morning I was feeling anything but 'contented'. There must be few in whose ministry there are not many moments when faith burns low, when the dimensions of what we are up against seem so much vaster than the dimensions of Grace. God seems very far away. Full of self-pity, coming down from the Cross, we murmur to ourselves 'My God, my God, why hast thou forsaken me?'

Well, on that Good Friday morning, I suddenly realized what, of course, I had always known, that Jesus did *not* come down from the Cross. Without a fraction of self-pity, though with most genuine bewilderment, *while still on the Cross*, he called out to his Father—invisible, intangible in that darkness, yet present to his faith—'My God, my God, why hast thou forsaken me?'

As I thought about those words, so very, very difficult to fit into any comfortable theory of the Atonement, I began in a small way not to understand any doctrine but to realize a little of why the Collect described Jesus as being 'contented' —'contented to be betrayed . . . given up . . . and to suffer death upon the Cross'.

He was 'contented' so it seemed to me [thus thinking] for three reasons. The *first* ground of contentment was that he was in the way of obedience. The decisive encounter with temptation had been made in the garden of Gethsemane—'Father, all things are possible unto thee: take away this cup from me: nevertheless not what I will, but what thou wilt' (Mark 14.36, AV).

The dictionary derives the word 'contented' from a Latin source which means, in its original sense, 'bounded in one's desires', hence 'satisfied'. The bounding of his desire was the Father's will—'I am come . . . not to do mine own will, but the will of him that sent me' (John 6.38, AV). 'My satisfaction, my meat,' said Jesus, 'is to do the will of him that sent me, and to finish his work' (John 4.34, AV).

Obedience, for Jesus, was always an immensely positive attitude to life. It was the discovery of the purposefulness of things and the harnessing of himself to that purposefulness. This is what lies at the heart of all his talk about the kingdom of God, or more accurately, the kingship of God. For him that kingship was the most real fact of all. Obedience was living in touch with reality. So to live and so to die was contentment.

In the *second* place, so at least meditation would suggest, Jesus was 'contented' because there on the Cross he was himself entering finally into the ultimate experience of being Man, the death-grapple with the last enemy. He who became Man for men had to taste to the very full the mystery of pain and suffering and sin, being made 'one with the sinfulness of men' (II Cor. 5.21), and one with men in his death. Out of that experience of complete identification with us he asked the question which sooner or later is asked by every human heart—'Why? Why? Why? What does it all mean?' There on the Cross in that cry of dereliction he was most surely 'made like unto his brethren' (Heb. 2.17, AV).

But his 'contentment' spelt more even than that. A *third* understanding is surely presented by the probability, even if we cannot claim the certainty, that our Lord so interpreted the prophecy of Isaiah about the suffering servant as to see in it a reference to himself. Isaiah said of that mysterious sufferer that 'He shall see of the travail of his soul and shall be satisfied' (Isa. 53.11, AV). So it was a sure insight which made the writer of the Letter to the Hebrews say of the Captain of our Salvation that 'for the joy that was set before him, he endured the Cross, despising the shame' (Heb. 12.2, AV).

We may surely say then that the word 'contentment' is rightly used in our Collect and not least as to his certainty about the outcome of the Cross, 'I, if I be lifted up . . . will draw all men unto me' (John 12.32, AV).

In the poem, 'The White Peace', Fiona MacLeod has these lines:

> It lies not on the sunlit hill
>   Nor on the sunlit plain:
> Nor ever on any running stream
>   Nor on the unclouded main—
>
> But sometimes, through the Soul of Man
>   Slow moving o'er his pain
> The moonlight of a perfect peace
>   Floods heart and brain.[1]

That hints at the 'contentment' of the Cross—his Cross and ours. And contentment has a great deal to say about being a healer as well as about being healed.

If we are at all to enter upon our own ministry of healing, to see the relevance of the Cross for that ministry, then we must first consider how our Lord endured suffering, and then, learning to suffer with him, be enabled by him to deal with the suffering of others.

As we confront the suffering of the world, and, if we have any imagination at all, feel completely overwhelmed by it, we will be prepared to realize the enormous complexity of suffering, a complexity which is reflected in the experience of Christ on the Cross.

[1] Fiona MacLeod, *Poems and Dramas* (Heinemann 1929), p. 70.

Consider for a moment the significance of the words of the inscription fastened to the Cross: 'Jesus of Nazareth, The King of the Jews' (John 19.19). There was all an Imperial Power's contempt for a subject people inscribed with those words. Here was another rebel dealt with, a warning to all who might still be meditating rebellion. Here was one more cross added to the thousands which had lined the roads of Galilee and Judaea in the years immediately before. Here was all the pathos of contemporary history, the agonies of frustrated nationalism, one more funeral of liberty.

There is a suggestive juxtaposition of sentences at the conclusion of St Luke's description of the Crucifixion. We read:

> Jesus gave a loud cry and said, 'Father, into thy hands I commit my spirit'; and with these words he died. The centurion saw it all, and gave praise to God. 'Beyond all doubt,' he said, 'this man was innocent.'

Was he the only one convinced and convicted by that cry? The words which follow seem to hint at something more—

> The crowd who had assembled for the spectacle, when they saw what had happened, went home beating their breasts. (Luke 23.46-48)

I do not think it is fanciful to assume that many of those who were in that crowd were also convinced of the innocence of Jesus, innocence at any rate of any crime justifying crucifixion. Yet, like the two on the road to Emmaus of whom St Luke tells us in the next chapter, there must have been many in that crowd who 'had been hoping that he was the man to liberate Israel' (Luke 24.21). So at the Cross we must see as one ingredient of the situation, one ingredient indeed of the suffering of Jesus himself, this awareness of men's political dreaming, of their disillusionment, and increasing bitterness, of that fatal spirit of racial intolerance and hate which a bare forty years ahead was to see Jerusalem ringed with thousands of crosses. The Cross was politically significant.

And it was culturally significant. That inscription was in three languages, Hebrew, Latin and Greek. On any reckoning that was symbolic of the three great forces which swayed the world of that day, Roman law, Greek culture and Hebrew religion, living always in an uneasy relationship. Tremendous human tensions are concealed beneath the three scripts in which the words 'Jesus of Nazareth, King of the Jews' were written.

The clash of cultures, then as now, adds its own meed to the suffering of individual men and women, as we see in the race conflicts of our own time.

We need to give full value to the political and cultural context of the Crucifixion for it is political and cultural facts and their economic correlations which are the context within which each individual lives his life. Sin, the sin with which Jesus was identified on the Cross, was not just the sin of individuals. It was also the corporate sinfulness of human society in all its innumerable forms. Our humanity's sickness calls for a very great healing.

Christ on the Cross prayed, indeed, for those who nailed him to it. And we must surely assume that beyond the rough soldiers, who were acting only under orders, our Lord's prayer for forgiveness was more deeply concerned with him who had given orders, Pilate, and beyond him the accusers, the chief priests: in the shadows behind them the man Judas, and likewise all the others who, when the test came, 'forsook him and fled' and even denied that they knew the Man. So all-encompassing was that prayer for forgiveness, so universal was the political, cultural and human situation at the Cross, so relevant to all times, that we know that in a profound sense we were all at the Cross —and all our circumstances, political, economic, cultural, social, come within the circle of its concern.

We must keep this all-embracing character of the Cross, its social no less than its individual relevance, in mind if we are to understand its healing power and recognize the range of our ministry of healing.

Keeping this wide range of our terms of reference in mind, we can afford to look more narrowly at the ministry of healing as it is committed to each one of us. Is it a suggestion altogether wide of the mark to say that one reason why Jesus was such a wonderful healer was that he was such a wonderful patient? That suggestion has, perhaps, something to say to us, lest we think of our ministry as being a 'stooping down' to people. A patient lies 'looking up' to others. The Jesus who looked down from his Cross had first knelt before his disciples and looked up into their faces, even while he washed their feet.

We arrive at this same point from another angle if we consider the words in Hebrews 2.18: 'Since he himself has passed through the test of suffering, he is able to help those who are meeting their test now.'

Again in Hebrews we read:

> Son though he was, he learned obedience in the school of suffering, and, once perfected, became the source of eternal salvation for all who obey him. (Heb. 5.8-9)

And the New Testament is very clear that this experience of being a patient, and so qualifying to be a healer, is an experience in which we are meant to share, so that we may become qualified.

> Christ also suffered for us, leaving us an example, that ye should follow his steps. (I Peter 2.21, AV)

Provided we do not press the figure too far, it is legitimate to find in that first Epistle of St Peter the idea of 'salvation by sympathy'—remembering that the root meaning of sympathy is 'to suffer with'. We might well call it healing by empathy—the projecting of one's own personality into, and so fully understanding, the other person. This, of course, is another road back to the meaning of the Incarnation.

Our subject must take us a little further. For at the Cross we see the full meaning of the Incarnation and that for two reasons. At the Cross we are confronted with a Person. But we are also confronted with many persons. Incarnation means life in a network of relationships. And the Cross is nothing if not a pattern of relationships. Never forgetting the supreme relationship of Jesus with his heavenly Father, we see at the Cross

Jesus and his human mother
Jesus and his friends, some nearby, some a little way off
Jesus and his enemies
Jesus and his unwitting and perhaps unwilling executioners
Jesus and his neighbours on their crosses
and, if the previous argument has been well sustained,
Jesus and ourselves.

Here, as we have already seen, though in more impersonal terms, the great tides of human history flow through the channels of individual exponents of Roman justice, Greek wisdom, Jewish piety. Here we see the great forces of evil concentrated in individuals with their fears, jealousies, treacheries, hatreds. Here we see problems as persons, persons themselves as the problems. It is important to keep this perspective. For we are not called to redeem evil, to heal sickness. We can only redeem evil men and women, heal the sick. Always, then, our way into the problems of our time is through persons—we go to heal persons, and through them deal with situations. This is not to evade the fact that many situations, not a few of the power-structures of our time for instance, are so apparently impersonal, do so depersonalize those involved in them, that it is difficult to find a person through whom to gain entrance. But what persons have created persons can re-create. Our task in such circumstances may be like a long-protracted siege, with continual mining operations. We may have to change the attitudes of mind of great numbers of people before this or that power-structure becomes humane. There may be no individual we can pin-point as an object of healing, but only a widely diffused climate of opinion. Yet the approach still remains a personal one.

An analogy may help us to see this point more clearly. In his book, *The Meaning of Persons,* Paul Tournier writes of the pressures on the modern medical profession. After speaking of the growth of 'social' medicine, and the new problems that raises for the doctor and the nurse, he says,

> On consideration one sees that the solution does not lie so much in institutions as in the attitude of the doctor. However much of a specialist or a scientist he be, he can still be human if in his personal and spiritual life he retains the sense of the person. Then he will understand that the deepest and the universal suffering of men is that which each one carries in the secrecy of his heart, and which throughout his life compromises his health of body and mind. It is a suffering which is not revealed in a moment in an atmosphere of mechanization, nor can it be got rid of by means of hastily-scribbled prescriptions.[1]

It is not perhaps out of order to add that this kind of suffering will not be revealed in a moment in the confessional either, nor can it be got rid of by any rule of thumb application of principles of moral theology. Under the pressure of time and circumstance all ministry can become mechanical, that is to say sub-human. Not so is healing mediated to those who are sick. Making men every whit whole is a profoundly personal ministry of healing.

In some fashion or another Paul's experience as described in Romans 7 is the experience of everyman, whether we define the struggle in terms of law or conscience or in the language of Freud and Jung. As healers our responsibility is to recognize that unless we have unlocked that secret room we have not really discharged our obedience to the divine command 'Go, heal'.

Our ministry is to the whole man. To heal means to make every whit whole. We can be satisfied with nothing less than a full atonement in which the man or the woman is made one with God, with neighbour, with environment and with

[1] Paul Tournier, *The Meaning of Persons* (SCM Press 1957), pp. 44-5.

the inner self. Health, wholeness, integrity, holiness belong together.

But full atonement, full healing, can never be an isolating experience, for the individual who is healed is always a person-in-relationship, in a whole complex web of relationships. Often it is some breakdown in one or another of these relationships which is the precipitating cause of the illness, the contriving source of debility. Healing, that is to say, has a direct bearing on the corporate life of man. It is of the utmost importance that we know ourselves and know those to whom we would minister healing, that all alike are persons-in-relationship. If those relationships are wrong there is trouble all round. Reconciliation is vital if there is to be real peace, if life is really to be worth living. In our ministry, then, we have to be sensitive to the maladjustments in the common life of society as these impinge on the individual—maladjustments within the family circle, in the social order, in political life, in the relation of man to the world of nature. The ecology of the patient has a direct bearing on his psychology.

There remains one further New Testament emphasis relevant to the ministry of healing, an emphasis which, in the profoundest way, is linked to the significance of the incarnate life of our Lord and to its culmination on the Cross. Healing, just because it is so many-sided an activity, is best understood as a group ministry. Modern medicine illustrates this in most dramatic fashion because, behind the individual physician or surgeon, there is always a group of people, chemists, biologists, pathologists, and many others, whose contributions to diagnosis, to cure, to after-care are indispensable. All too easily we enfeeble our own ministry and the total witness of the Church by imagining that the minds and souls of men are to be dealt with any differently from their bodies. Indeed, we sometimes forget, as the practitioners of scientific medicine for their part sometimes forget, that man is intended to be a unity. Full atonement is a physical, mental and spiritual phenomenon. The most thorough achievement of healing calls in our human experience for a many-sided ministry which corresponds with the many-sidedness of our beings and of our relationships.

This has something to say about the meaning of the Cross. While our Lord did indeed make 'one full, perfect and sufficient sacrifice' and made it in his own person; while it must always remain true that he, and he alone, was the Proper Man: yet we misunderstand the nature of his humanity if we think of him as being any more an isolated individual than we are ourselves. To an extent beyond our capacity to imagine he was all mankind. This is the inwardness of what Paul attempted to express in his description of him as, in effect, a second Adam (Romans 5). The infinite significance of the Cross derives from the infinitely significant Person of the Crucified.

Nor is it anything but a sequel to the act of atonement on the Cross that the means by which that atonement is to be made known, interpreted, demonstrated and made available is through the Body of Christ—the community of those who have been made one with him in a shared death and resurrection, which oneness is signified in the New Testament by Baptism (Rom. 6.1-11).

The whole New Testament bears witness to this understanding of the corporate relationship of Christ and his Church. There is true inspiration behind the way in which the New English Bible makes St Paul address the Christians of Ephesus, Philippi and Colossae as being 'incorporate in Christ Jesus'. In turn this has a direct bearing on our ministry of healing. This can be illustrated from the way in which St Paul brings his great argument in Galatians to a conclusion. In Chapter 5 he has reached his climax by describing the Christian life as life in the Spirit and has summoned his readers to walk in the Spirit. The Apostle, however, knows his Galatians, as he would appear to know us also! So he goes straight from the assumption that the Christian does live by the Spirit to the observed fact that the Christian also grieves the Spirit by the way in which he so easily breaks fellowship with his fellow Christians. Then there follows a passage of great tenderness which takes us to the very heart of the Beloved Community. He writes:

> If a man should do something wrong, my brothers, on a sudden impulse, you who are endowed with the Spirit must set him right again very gently. Look to yourself, each one of you: you may be tempted too. (Gal. 6.1-2)

Paul is concerned with the disrupting power of sin, not just with the way in which it disintegrates the personality of the individual, but the way in which it breaks up the common life. His prescription for the treatment is worth noting. It is gentleness born of humility. The breach is to be healed. The wound in the life of the fellowship is to be bound up. All that we have seen of the relation of forgiveness with healing is here involved. Without making too much of the point, it is interesting to note that the verb translated 'set him right' (in the AV 'restore') is *katartidzo*, which is also the technical medical term for the setting of a broken limb. The association of the adverb 'gently' with the word to 'set him right' would suggest that the medical use of the term may not have been foreign to Paul's thought in the moment of writing.

Another New Testament illustration comes in Paul's first letter to the Corinthians. He has been deeply distressed to hear that the very unity of the Church is in danger of being disrupted by schism, with the grave corollary that, so disrupted, the Church could not minister healing to a disrupted world. The long and tragic story of Christian disunity is seen in its beginnings. To these divided Christians Paul writes:

> I appeal to you, my brothers, in the name of our Lord Jesus Christ: agree among yourselves, and avoid divisions; be firmly joined in unity of mind and thought. (I Cor. 1.10)

What Paul is calling for is the restoration of harmony, the at-one-ment among brethren for whom at-one-ment with God has been established. As he has just reminded them: 'It is God himself who called you to share in the life of his

Son, Jesus Christ our Lord; and God keeps faith' (v. 9). The breach must be healed. The surgical analogy is perhaps not present here as obviously as in the Galatian passage, but it is interesting that the same verb *katartidzo* is used, which is here translated 'firmly joined in unity'.

Those are just two New Testament illustrations whose inner meaning can be traced directly back to the place of atonement, to the Cross, where, in the Person of the Crucified, we know that God and man are at one, that man is at home with God. And as we find ourselves being drawn up by grace to find ourselves new made on that Cross, we discover that we are looking with new eyes upon our fellow men and the world which God has given us to share with them. In this tremendous encounter we discover our own sinfulness in all its infinite ramifications which divide us within ourselves and help us to be sources of division in the lives of others. To that sin we are to die so that being unclothed by death we may be clothed upon with the new life of the risen Christ, in the power of which alone we can 'go heal'.

> The stars wailed when the reed was born,
> And heaven wept at the birth of the thorn:
> Joy was pluckt like a flower and torn,
> For Time foreshadowed Good Friday morn.
>
> But the stars laughed like children free
> And heaven was hung with the rainbow's glee
> When at Easter Sunday, so fair to see,
> Time bowed before Eternity.[1]

Almighty God, we beseech thee graciously to behold this thy family, for which our Lord Jesus Christ was 'contented' to be betrayed and given up into the hands of wicked men, and to suffer death upon the Cross, who now liveth and reigneth with thee and the Holy Ghost ever one God, world without end.

[1] Fiona MacLeod, 'Easter', *Poems and Dramas* (Heinemann 1929), p. 278.

6

The Cross in our Ministry
of Teaching

JESUS CHRIST lived the Cross before he died upon it.
His living was the teaching upon which the Cross itself
threw the light of a vast illumination. Unless we can see this
and understand that all Christ's living was a dying, we shall
not plumb the depths of what is involved for us in our
ministry of teaching. For if the Cross stands at the centre
of history, as Christians believe; if it is the central key to
understanding the nature of God, the dilemma of man, the
mystery of life and death; then we have to expound its
meaning as the way in which all men are meant to live and
die. This carries with it the implication that we too must live
it if we are to teach it.

Now, if we are to be at all realistic about the meaning of
the Cross as the symbol of living quite as much as of dying,
we must begin by evacuating it of drama. It is only as a
sacrament of the commonplace that we can discover the
Cross of living. The lad who could say in a moment of
exaltation 'Did you not know that I was bound to be in my
Father's house?' was the one who could go back to the
small-town life in Nazareth and there continue to be 'under
authority' (Luke 2.49-51). The grown man, conscious of his
calling, pondering the mystery of his destiny, was the one
who was for ever at men's beck and call and knew times
when the pressure of demand was such that there was 'no
chance to eat' (Mark 3.20); and, being thus busy with the
common people's common needs, was assumed by his family

to be on the verge of a break-down, as we would call it.
Continually on the move, he had 'nowhere to lay his head'
(Matt. 8.20). Yet all the while he was fulfilling his role as a
teacher, concentrating increasingly on the few, but taking
every opportunity that presented itself of explaining life's
inwardness to the crowds, right up to the end. Infinitely
patient with the obtuse and obstructive, he never lost sight
of his objective which was indeed to be, what one perceptive
visitor recognized, 'a teacher sent by God' (John 3.2).

It was, indeed, supremely as a teacher that Jesus caught
men's attention. His healing ministry was, so it would seem,
incidental to his teaching ministry and not the other way
round. Almost we might say that his healings were illustrations of his teachings. There is some importance in getting
the picture clear, else we shall be preoccupied with the
dramatic element that no doubt was present in the healings,
and overlook the long-drawn-out, endless, exhausting because demanding, activity of the teacher. And if we remember just how obtuse most of his hearers were, we can glimpse
the Cross behind the words, repeated to his inner circle so
often, 'Do you not understand even yet?' (Matt. 16.9);
'Are you as dull as the rest?' (Mark 7.18). Is there anything
more poignant in the story of Jesus than the apparent in-
ability of his closest friends to glimpse the meaning of his
life and words?

But there is surely also another hidden Cross in that
strange and perplexing passage in St Mark where Jesus says
to his disciples:

> To you the secret of the kingdom of God has been given;
> but to those who are outside everything comes by way of
> parables, so that (as Scripture says) they may look and look,
> but see nothing; they may hear and hear but understand
> nothing; otherwise they might turn to God and be forgiven.
> (Mark 4.11-12)

At first showing the statement makes intolerable reading. It
seems in flagrant contradiction to all we know of Jesus.
What meaning can it have when put beside 'Come to me,

all whose work is hard, whose load is heavy; and I will give you relief', to quote the New English Bible's forceful rendering of the first of the Comfortable Words in the Holy Communion Service (Matt. 11.28)?

The explanation surely lies in the inwardness of the true art of teaching which is not to overawe with knowledge but to draw out the capacity of the learners so that, looking, they really see. This involves infinite patience, for the teacher the crucifixion which always refuses the short cut, the easy way of cramming with facts instead of encouraging thought. For Jesus was 'a teacher sent by God' and he had something to reveal about God.

A recent commentary on St Mark's Gospel can help us to see what this perplexing passage means:

> God's self-revelation is indirect and veiled. . . . No outwardly compelling evidence of divine glory illumines the ministry of Jesus. It is a necessary part of the gracious self-abasement of the Incarnation that the Son of God should submit to conditions under which his claim to authority cannot but appear altogether problematic and paradoxical. In the last hours of his life his incognito deepens until in the helplessness, nakedness and agony of the Cross, abandoned by God and man, he becomes the absolute antithesis of everything the world understands by divinity and by kingship. But this veiledness is not simply designed to prevent men from recognizing the truth. . . . God's self-revelation is veiled, in order that men may be left sufficient room in which to make a personal decision. A real turning to God or repentance . . . is made possible by the inward divine enabling of the Holy Spirit . . ., but would be rendered impossible by the external compulsion of a manifestation of the unveiled divine majesty. The revelation is veiled for the sake of man's freedom to believe.[1]

For a full explanation of this difficult passage, reference should be made to Cranfield's Commentary. Enough, how-

[1] C. E. B. Cranfield, *The Gospel According to St Mark*, The Cambridge Greek Testament Commentary (Cambridge University Press 1963), pp. 157-8.

ever, has here been indicated to show the Cross in our Lord's ministry of teaching, as the utter self-abnegation of the true teacher who will not compel but only elicit. To know and to know the joy of knowing and to withhold that knowledge except it be come by rightly, this is the pain of the teacher, the Cross in education.

Something of this can be seen in letters I received some years ago from a missionary, teaching in a secondary school for girls in Africa. She wrote:

> If anyone asked me what I had achieved in the last three years I should find it very difficult to reply, and I could easily be persuaded on the level of argument that therefore I might as well not be here.

Anyone with a real passionate belief in the ministry of teaching will quickly feel the potential sense of futility in the mind of that teacher, the kind of despair which so easily leads so many to give up. That teacher hasn't given up.

Later in the same letter she continued:

> But beyond the level of argument I know that the work of a teacher is to be *there* and to put the truth of God in the way of those he teaches and leave them free to discover the wonder and marvel of it for themselves, if possible without noticing who put it in their way.

That teacher-disciple of Jesus was providing a contemporary illustration of the words just quoted from the Commentator on Mark 4.11-12.

The same writer in another letter a year later had this further piece of experience to record:

> Teaching is the same the world over, I suppose. It often seems to be more demanding out here, where shortage of staff is an ever-present strain on the ones who are there. Even so, you do what you do because it is in you and you must, and it has its rewards, though seldom at once, and seldom comprehensible to others. By rewards, I mean knowing that something of eternal value has been created in the meetings between teacher and taught and the great Teacher

Himself. But they are inexpressible, intangible things, understood only in the experience itself.

Would it be too much to say that we find here an echo, faint perhaps but real, of those words about the great Teacher which come in Hebrews 12.2: 'Jesus who, for the sake of the joy that lay ahead of him, endured the cross'?

I have thus linked together the great Teacher and one of his teaching-disciples of set purpose, by way of a reminder that in so far as we are teachers, we are called to share in his ministry of teaching—its glory and its pain, its rewards and its Cross. Our theme, however, must take us deeper still. There is a theology of teaching which can be understood only in so far as we see how our Lord in living the Cross taught its meaning, explained what it revealed.

We are all familiar with the symbolism of the Cross—the upright shaft and the cross-beam—betokening the vertical relationship of man to God and the horizontal relationship of man with man. And we rightly see upon the Cross One who was perfectly identified with God and also with all mankind.

Inevitably, perhaps, and perhaps rightly as of the divine intention, it is the 'horizontal' of the Cross which speaks home to us. For after all, we are men. And it means much to us that his arms were there stretched out as if offering a universal embrace. He willed the embrace. Man's tragedy is that by nailing him there man refused the embrace. His will was to overcome our refusal making his acceptance of our rejection the means of our restoration.

But more than this, we find in the 'horizontal' of the Cross that which speaks to us directly and immediately with a challenge we cannot easily evade. The relationship of man with man is our daily experience. We are but rarely conscious of God. We are all the time acutely aware of each other, in embarrassment if not in pleasure, in hatred if not in love. We do not need to be argued into seeing the force of the words,

> If a man says, 'I love God', while hating his brother, he is a liar. If he does not love the brother whom he has seen, it cannot be that he loves God whom he has not seen. (I John 4.20)

and again from the same letter

> If a man has enough to live on, and yet when he sees his brother in need shuts up his heart against him, how can it be said that love for God dwells in him. (I John 3.17)

In the 'horizontal' of the Cross we recognize Jesus as 'The Man for Others', know instinctively that that is our vocation too, that that is the way to live even if the cross of life should lead to the cross in dying. What, however, we must realize, if we are not totally to misunderstand Jesus and misinterpret his Cross in its deepest and ultimate significance, is that behind, in and through the 'Man for Others' was the 'Man for God'. The 'horizontal' of the Cross can only bear the weight of redemption because it is fixed to the 'vertical'.

In his book, *Mystery of Man*, Professor Jeffreys writes of the necessary assumption which has to be made if we are to make sense of the ideal of universal fellowship—if, that is to say, we dare to believe in the harmony of humanity against all the evidence! Professor Jeffreys says:

> There is a sense in which being loved is prior to loving. Love needs to be evoked, and we cannot love to order. Yet it is of the essence of love not to be limited or exclusive, but to be ever outgoing. Therefore there is a sense in which we must love the whole before we can love the part; otherwise there cannot be the right attitude towards a newly experienced individual or group. The right *approach* implies a prior assumption of acceptance. This situation spells frustration unless there is a universal resource of love available, in response to which we can make that prior acceptance which conditions our individual responses. The assumption of a loving God makes sense of that dilemma. 'Love one another, for love is of God.' Indeed we cannot love any human individual truly unless we love God, since our love can be

purified of selfishness, possessiveness, only if we have the ultimate assurance of being possessed by God. Only then can we love without *arrière pensée*.[1]

For our purpose we must, so I believe, stress what Professor Jeffreys calls the 'prior assumption', the assumption that we are 'accepted', that there is a 'universal resource of love available'. This is the vertical dimension of the Cross and this it was which lay at the very centre of our Lord's living of the Cross. Tillich has finely expressed this in unforgettable words:

> You are accepted. *You are accepted*, accepted by that which is greater than you, and the name of which you do not know. Do not ask for the name now; perhaps you will find it later. Do not try to do anything now; perhaps later you will do much. Do not seek for anything; do not perform anything; do not intend anything. *Simply accept the fact that you are accepted.*[2]

That is very near the heart of the Gospel and it is directly related to the 'vertical' dimension of the Cross. This it is which gives that perfect freedom to enter into the experience of the Cross seen in its horizontal embrace of the neighbour and of all mankind.

Now it is about this vertical dimension that Jesus was primarily concerned in his *teaching*, a teaching which was illustrated by his *actions* in an outgoing love to wherever there was human need, need of healing whether of body, mind or spirit.

His *teaching* had three main strands relevant to our theme, and these three strands are illuminated by the Cross on Calvary as they also prefigure it and in each case show that the teaching was based on a living experience which was itself an experience of the Cross.

[1] M. C. V. Jeffreys, *Mystery of Man* (Sir Isaac Pitman and Sons Ltd. 1957), p. 46.
[2] Paul Tillich, *The Shaking of the Foundations* (Pelican Books 1962), p. 163.

The *first* of these strands is what Jesus has to say about God understood as Father. We have earlier seen the importance given in the Bible, not least in the Old Testament, to the thought of God as 'Father'. But the immediate relevance of the Fatherhood of God to the teaching of Jesus, and its association with the Cross, is only to be found in the experience of Jesus, and in the teaching which was an expression of that experience. What is quite clear from the Gospels is that his experience of God as Father was for Jesus the dominating experience of his whole life from the Baptism to his Crucifixion.

At the Baptism we have clearly an experience of calling to a distinctive ministry and as such it is one in the succession of calls recorded of others in the prophetic tradition. But there is here a significant difference. With the prophets of the Old Testament the vision and the voice were a call to action. But as T. W. Manson says:

> With the vision and the voice at the Baptism the case is otherwise: Jesus receives an assurance, the essence of which is contained in the declaration: 'Thou art my Son'. What is given here is not a task to be performed or a message to be delivered, but a status and a relation. At the very outset it is indicated that the central theme in his ministry will be what he *is* rather than what he *says*. As the ministry continues the message becomes plainer and the task more obvious; but both message and task are still conditioned by the primary fact of sonship.[1]

To *be* rather than to *say*—those words remind us that the deepest lessons are caught not taught. How tragically often it is true of us whose ministry is to teach, that what we are speaks so loudly that men and women cannot hear what we say. Jesus was *someone* before he taught *anything*.

This *being* of Jesus was a life of dependence, of subordination. It was in a life-time of doing his Father's will, of seeking nothing for himself or by himself, and therefore of

[1] T. W. Manson, *The Teaching of Jesus—Studies of its Form and Content* (Cambridge University Press 1959), pp. 103-4.

continually saying 'no' to himself, that he came to the test of Gethsemane. And there in great fear and trembling, in a moment of near despair at the apparent failure of his mission, at a time when all life's physical, mental, and spiritual resources were at their lowest, he could both shrink from the ordeal ahead and yet say:

> Abba, Father, all things are possible to thee; take this cup away from me. Yet not what I will, but what thou wilt. (Mark 14.36)

Such was the *being* of Jesus. And it was out of that *being* that his teaching sprang. For the most part, his teaching about the Fatherhood of God was conveyed to the inner circle of his disciples. Far and away the greater number of references to the Fatherhood of God in the Synoptics (though not in the Fourth Gospel) are references in conversations which Jesus had with his disciples.

It is to committed disciples that the 'Spirit of your Father' (Matt. 10.20) is promised, when they are on trial for their discipleship—a significant promise in view of the experience of the Spirit at Jesus's Baptism. Of this T. W. Manson writes:

> It is not that Jesus receives an inspired message, but that the spiritual source of all inspiration takes possession of him, so that when he speaks it is not that he repeats words given to him but that the Spirit of his Father speaks in him.[1]

And Jesus would say, 'As is the Master shall the servant be'. The association of experiences referred to is too close to be doubted.

Again, it was to disciples, to committed men, that he gave the prayer which was to be the pattern of all their praying. They were bidden approach God as Father with the same utter confidence with which Jesus could address him, as he did when the seventy disciples returned with their enthusiastic report of the success of their mission (Luke

[1] T. W. Manson, op. cit., p. 107.

10.17-22), and as he could also do in almost exactly contrary circumstances when St Matthew records the same words in the context of the failure of a mission (Matt. 11.20-27). Here is a contrast in its own way as dramatic as that between the joy at the Baptism and the agony of Gethsemane. But always and at all times and in all circumstances it is 'Father'. So he was and so he taught.

Yet if it be true, and the evidence certainly points that way, that most of the teaching of Jesus about God as Father was not broadcast but rather conveyed to a small group: a group to whom its meaning could be interpreted beyond the risk of misunderstanding, who could in fact begin at least to glimpse the Cross at the heart of Fatherhood and of Sonship: that is not the whole story.

It was to a wider company that Jesus taught the disconcerting lesson recorded in Matthew 12.50 when his family tried to interrupt his teaching. At that moment he said, pointing to the disciples but addressing the crowd, 'Whoever does the will of my heavenly Father is my brother, my sister, my mother.' It is not fanciful to say that those words might well have come almost anywhere in the Fourth Gospel. A close parallel can be found in John 12.26 when again in a crowd we hear him say, 'If anyone serves me, he must follow me; where I am, my servant will be. Whoever serves me will be honoured by my Father.'

Jesus *was* what he *was* for all men. The strategy of his ministry might lie in giving intensive teaching to a limited number, but there was no limitation in the intention of his mission. It was his way of preparing for its extension to the ends of the earth.

We may add that it was to a very general audience, including some who were critical and hostile, that Jesus told the story of the Prodigal Son. That God is like a Father is implicit in that story. Scarcely less implicit is the suffering heart of God, so understood.

The *second* strand in the teaching of Jesus which is illuminated by the Cross of Calvary, but which also throws its own meaning forward and thus prepares for that Cross, is the teaching of Jesus about the kingdom of God.

The great prophets of the Old Testament had established beyond all question that at the heart of the Jewish faith there should be a conviction about the universal sovereignty of God. The leader of a desert tribe, the ruler of a settled community, in either case possessed by his people as much as their possessor, one who was as much bound by his covenant with them as they were by their covenant with him, has now become a universal Lord. Isaiah sees him 'high and lifted up sitting upon a throne'. Micaiah the son of Imlah sees him on his throne with all the hosts of heaven standing around him. Ezekiel in his vision sees God in his throne-chariot. This universal Lord is independent of any special relation with Israel. In a superb passage one of the greatest of all the prophets describes the Sovereign of the Universe as completely transcending this little world. Here, indeed, is the vision of a Space Age:

> Behold, the nations are like a drop from a bucket, and are accounted as the dust on the scales; behold, he takes up the isles like fine dust. . . . All the nations are as nothing before him, they are accounted by him as less than nothing and emptiness. (Isa. 40.15, 17, RSV)

This conviction about the overall sovereignty of God must be understood as the background conviction in the mind of Jesus when he talks about the kingdom of God. The new element which is introduced by Jesus is that this kingdom is envisaged not as a territorial dominion, however, transcending individual nations or even the globe itself. Rather it becomes in his hands the omnipresent kingship of God.

But we must go further than this. As such it could be a theological inference from the great prophets, and as such an inference it had already been drawn and applied by the best of the rabbis. For Jesus, however, the kingdom of God was nothing less than the sphere in which he himself lived and moved and had his being.

His preaching of the kingdom is not just the pointing of his hearers to some happy state in the future, when the will of God will be perfectly realized; it is primarily the living of a life of complete loyalty to God and unquestioning obedience to his will here and now.[1]

And Jesus began by accepting this rule of God in his own life. As Manson says again: 'The essence of his preaching of the kingdom is in the words "Thy will be done": all the rest is commentary.'[2]

And it was because, for him, obedience to the rule of God was the touchstone of all his actions that he could be so uncompromising in his demand that men should follow him. In following him they were in fact entering the kingdom, because they were thereby involved with him in a common obedience to the King of the kingdom.

Thinking thus of the King, of kingship and the kingdom, Jesus had one supreme object in view, to persuade men to choose God as the sole object of their loyalty. To do that was to enter the kingdom.

To that absolute demand men put up an absolute resistance. At the best they counted the cost and went away sorrowful for they had great possessions. At the worst they felt that Jesus was a threat to the whole social order, and they found it expedient that one man should die for the people.

Saying 'Yes' to God must involve the Cross. For to say 'Yes' to God, as Jesus revealed him, is to say 'No' to every other object of worship. And that denial involves the vested interest of self, family, society and nation. Crucifixion can, of course, take many forms. In the first-century Jerusalem it involved a wooden gibbet. In twentieth-century England it could mean what Studdert Kennedy described in his poem 'Indifference'.

When Jesus came to Birmingham they simply passed him by,
They never hurt a hair of him, they only let him die;

---

[1] T. W. Manson, op. cit., p. 161.   [2] Ibid.

> For men had grown more tender, and they would not give
> him pain,
> They only just passed down the street, and left him in the
> rain.[1]

However it be, 'the Man for Others' dies for others, now as then, precisely because he cannot do anything else. It is the law of the Cross. On Calvary men thought they were crucifying the King of the Jews. Actually they were enthroning, high and lifted up, the King of the Universe. On the Cross the kingdom came in power. It is the deepest of all Christian convictions that there, as in all his living, all his daily dying, God was in Christ reconciling the world to himself. So the kingdom came and comes.

Would we understand the manner of its coming today, we must look at the *third* strand in the teaching of Jesus and see what he meant by that title under which he most preferred to be known—'The Son of Man'.

Much painstaking theological research has gone into the attempt to understand what our Lord meant by his use of this enigmatic title of 'The Son of Man'. Perhaps we are on the surest ground if we recognize that it was deliberately enigmatic, and that he was content then, as he is content still, that his disciples should bring to its interpretation each his own understanding and obedience, only refusing to be dogmatically self-confident that the understanding is exclusively right, the obedience necessarily of one kind. One thing is certain. The title did not denote a separating of himself from the sons of men. Simply and immediately it identified him with them. This has far-reaching consequences.

Two points may be suggested as worthy of consideration in our relation of this strand of his teaching to our own ministry of teaching in the light of the Cross. The first of these is the reminder that the great majority of the occasions on which Jesus is recorded as using this title come after the

[1] G. Studdert Kennedy, *The Unutterable Beauty* (Hodder and Stoughton 1930), p. 24.

scene at Caesarea Philippi and Peter's confession of his belief that Jesus was the Messiah. And it was from that moment that Jesus seems to have concentrated on preparing his inner circle of disciples for his Passion. It would hardly be an exaggeration to say that the very title, 'Son of Man', is a title linked directly with the idea of suffering. This is markedly true of St Mark and St Luke. And even in St Matthew's Gospel, where a different order of events is followed, most of the instances of the use of 'The Son of Man' are in a context which either implies the Passion or looks forward to events connected with the End (cf. Matt. 10.23; 11.19; 12.40; 13.41).

We may say then that when he used this title Jesus was not only using words which left men free to interpret him as they wished, if necessary to misinterpret him, but he was also using it to describe himself as *he was to be discovered*.

This is important, for what was to be discovered was an identification with men which was absolute, an identification which fully included suffering and death. Here is the ground upon which we can say:

> ours is not a high priest unable to sympathize with our weaknesses, but one who, because of his likeness to us, has been tested every way, only without sin. Let us therefore boldly approach the throne of our gracious God, where we may receive mercy and in his grace find timely help. (Heb. 4.15-16)

The second point for consideration is the remarkable amount of evidence from Caesarea Philippi onwards that

> what was in the mind of Jesus was that he and his followers *together* should share that destiny which he describes as the Passion of the Son of Man: that he and they *together* should be the Son of Man, the Remnant that saves by service and self-sacrifice, the organ of God's redemptive purpose in the world.[1]

[1] T. W. Manson, op. cit., p. 231. For the full argument sustaining this thesis, see pp. 231-6.

We very easily take the constant refrain, 'Anyone who wishes to be a follower of mine must leave self behind; he must take up his cross, and come with me' (Mark 8.34), and interpret it figuratively. Was Thomas right after all in the insight which led him to say, when the last journey to Jerusalem was begun, 'Let us also go that we may die with him' (John 11.16)? Does this whole possibility shed a new light on St Paul's words:

> It is now my happiness to suffer for you. This is my way of helping to complete, in my poor human flesh, the full tale of Christ's afflictions still to be endured, for the sake of his body which is the Church. (Col. 1.24)

and again,

> As Christ's cup of suffering overflows, and we suffer with him, so also through Christ our consolation overflows. (II Cor. 1.5)

The Cross in our ministry of teaching? If we are to be cross-bearers, if we are to be true interpreters of the Cross, we too must see that we hold this threefold balance of truth, which we have been considering. *The Fatherhood of God* in the teaching of Jesus is a reminder that sonship must mean a way of *being* before anything is said, else what is said will simply not be understood, or wrongly understood and will properly be rejected. *The kingdom of God* in the teaching of Jesus was a summons to decision far more decisive, far more comprehensive than Elijah's challenge on Mount Carmel. *The Son of Man* in the teaching of Jesus at least points to this, that even when we have got our status right, even when we have made the great decision, 'the reward of faithfulness may be a crown of thorns'.

That is the teachers' charter. We have no authority to teach anything else.

7

The Cross in our Ministry of Evangelism

TO EVANGELIZE is to introduce people to Someone who is 'news', and 'good news' at that. So, in Christian tradition, it has always been. So it was that, on the day of Pentecost, Peter could arrest the attention of a crowd with the words:

> Men of Israel, listen to me: I speak of Jesus of Nazareth, a man singled out by God . . . you used heathen men to crucify and kill him. But God raised him to life again . . . repent and be baptized, everyone of you . . . and you will receive the gift of the Holy Spirit. For the promise is to you, and to your children, and to all who are far away, everyone whom the Lord our God may call. (Acts 2.22-24, 38-39)

So it was that Paul, assuming a mission to those who were indeed 'far away', not only in a geographical but in a cultural and racial sense also, came to Athens 'preaching about Jesus and the Resurrection' (Acts 17.18).

So, very easily, we find ourselves picturing the triumphant progress of the Christian Gospel as being something in the nature of things. We point to the astonishing fact that within three centuries the Cross, to which a Roman Governor condemned Jesus of Nazareth, became the sign in which a Roman Emperor could win a decisive victory over his enemies. Legend or not, the sequel to that victory was the fact that the Cross from that moment in the Western world ceased to be a gibbet and was transformed into jewelry. There was something astonishing about this.

Perhaps more astonishing still was the later achievement, by which the barbarian invaders of Rome were gradually persuaded of the *goodness* of what was certainly 'news' to them of a God who died and rose again.

And the story continues with that phenomenal outburst of energy from the end of the fifteenth century down to the end of the nineteenth century, when the peoples of Europe spread to the world's end, settling whole continents, ruling where settlement was uncongenial and holding 'the gorgeous East in fee'. Today we talk about imperialism and cultural aggression. But during these centuries this expansion looked like a mission of civilization and Christians saw it all in simple terms of the spread of the Gospel. In deep sincerity Christians have sung for over a hundred years,

> From many an ancient river,
>   From many a palmy plain,
> They call us to deliver
>   Their land from error's chain.

With a like faith we have also sung,

> March we forth in the strength of God with the banner of Christ unfurled,
> That the light of the glorious Gospel of truth may shine throughout the world.
> Fight we the fight with sorrow and sin, to set their captives free,
> That the earth may be filled with the glory of God as the waters cover the sea.

Not without some presumption, in choirs and places where they sing, there have echoed the words,

> Trumpet of God, sound high,
>   Till the hearts of the heathen shake,
> And the souls that in slumber lie
>   At the voice of the Lord awake,
> Till the fenced cities fall
>   At the blast of the Gospel call,
> Trumpet of God, sound high!

D

And it hasn't happened! Round how many Jerichos have we marched, and for how long, and there is not much sign of the walls even cracking, let alone falling down! The fight with sorrow and sin is going on, beyond doubt, but there is not much sign of the light of the glorious Gospel illuminating our world, otherwise than to the eye of faith. A very few of the world's peoples appear to be asking us Christians to deliver their land from error's chains. For the bulk of the world's peoples the supreme error from which they have sought deliverance is the error of alien rule. And they have broken their own chains. It is a disconcerting fact that many of them confuse the white man's rule with the Gospel that some white men brought to them.

Clearly something has gone wrong. Clearly there is a dimension of evangelism which has been inadequately stressed. Clearly we today have to undertake a reappraisal of our whole ministering of the Gospel.

The first point about which we need to be clear is that the Someone to whom we seek to introduce men is by no means immediately attractive. He never was. The Old Testament anticipation of him has proved a remarkable prophecy about the reaction of most men, most of the time :

> As many were astonished at him—his appearance was so marred, beyond human semblance, and his form beyond that of the sons of men—so shall he startle many nations; kings shall shut their mouths because of him . . . he had no form or comeliness that we should look at him, and no beauty that we should desire him. He was despised and rejected by men; a man of sorrows, and acquainted with grief; and as one from whom men hid their faces he was despised, and we esteemed him not. (Isa. 52.14-15; 53.2-3, RSV)

Why should we imagine that such a figure should do much more than startle men? Very early in the Church's experience of the Gospel the 'good news' about God which Jesus had proclaimed was being misunderstood and rejected as firmly as he had been misunderstood and rejected. Pentecost, we sometimes forget, ushered in persecution. Paul, that persecuting and much persecuted man, came early to an understanding of just how unattractive the Gospel was. For what he had to proclaim was 'Christ—yes, Christ nailed to the Cross'. And this was 'a stumbling-block to Jews and folly to Greeks'. Only to those who could hear deep in themselves the 'still sad music of humanity' and in its pain hear also the voice of the One who shared that sadness to the full, 'a man of sorrows and acquainted with grief'—only to those was there given to hear his call and to know in him 'the power and wisdom of God' (I Cor. 1.23-24). Paul, writing to other Christians many years later, had learnt to be able to say:

> It is now my happiness to suffer for you. This is my way of helping to complete, in my poor human flesh, the full tale of Christ's afflictions still to be endured. (Col. 1.24)

For Paul the Cross was not only the heart of his Gospel. It was an experience he had to share. 'To know Christ, and to experience the power of his resurrection' was, as he said elsewhere, 'to share his sufferings, in growing conformity with his death' (Phil. 3.10).

The Cross is not only the central theme of evangelism. It has to be the central experience of the evangelist. These are hard sayings, who can hear them? But if we recognize that this has been so from the beginning, that all attempts to evangelize which have diminished the emphasis upon the Cross have been spurious, we can both the better understand the erratic course of the Christian missionary enterprise down the centuries, and at the same time understand what is involved in our ministry of evangelism today.

For we too face the unattractiveness of the Gospel as being a major obstacle in the way of introducing people to Jesus Christ. From the point of view of vast numbers of people today Jesus is not news-worthy. In Western society, in what can without exaggeration be called the 'post-Christian' world, he is even stale news. That thought may shock

Christians but it is a fact with which they must come to terms.

Colin Wilson, the author of *The Outsider*,[1] wrote, in an autobiographical introduction to a later book, an explanation of what had been his intention in writing *The Outsider*. It was, he said, an attempt at 'a search for meaning in human life'. And he went on to explain his fundamental difficulty about Christianity: it was

> my failure to see any need for Christ. The need for God I could understand, and the need for religion; I could even sympathize with devotees like Suso or St Francis, who weave fantasies around the Cross, the nails, and all the other traditional symbols. But ultimately I could not accept the need for redemption by a Saviour. To pin down the idea of salvation to one point in space and time seemed a naïve kind of anthropomorphosis.

Canon Douglas Webster from whose book, *What is Evangelism?*, I have taken that quotation adds a comment. This difficulty of Colin Wilson's 'is revealing, for it is in effect a confession not only that the Church is irrelevant—which is taken for granted—but that even Christ is irrelevant'.[2]

The Christ does not seem to mean anything to many men and women in our contemporary world, in so far as that world is post-Christian, in which God is no more, and therefore in which his revelation in Christ has no meaning. 'Is it nothing to you, all you who pass by?' (Lamentations 1.12, RSV). To that question, traditionally read in its context during Holy Week, the answer is 'Nothing'. For the Christian there is indeed a Cross involved in living in a post-Christian society. He is ready enough to admit his own rejection by that society, for the more Christian he is the more he understands and sympathizes with those who reject

[1] Gollancz 1956.
[2] D. Webster, *What is Evangelism?* (Highway Press 1959), p. 48. The quotation is from Colin Wilson, *Religion and the Rebel* (Gollancz 1957), p. 39. Canon Webster's book is a most perceptive and penetrating answer to the question in its title.

him. He is after all a very poor advertisement of Christ. What is a real crucifixion for those concerned in the ministry of evangelism is not to be able to persuade men of 'the need for redemption by a Saviour', above all by such a Saviour. It is an inescapable part of the Cross in our ministry of evangelism, the cross we have to carry, that we cannot persuade men that the Cross has a meaning.

What is the Christian to say to men in this situation? I know no better answer than that offered by Canon Webster. Wrestling with the same problem over many years, he has come to a conclusion to which I believe we have all got to come as a preliminary to exercising among such people as we have in mind any evangelistic ministry at all. He writes:

> The modern intellectual is not unlike Job. He clings to his integrity, he suffers and he asks questions. It will be remembered that his friends with their easy words, their reasoned phrases, their glib dogmas and their safe distance from his existential situation, had no effect on him whatever. They were too ready to speak, too slow to listen. They never began to enter into Job's problem.

Webster adds:

> It is important that the Christian, especially the evangelist, should not play the role of Job's comforter to the modern intellectual of today. We cannot begin to evangelize these or any others until we listen, and we may have to listen for years.[1]

The mark of a good listener is that he respects the integrity of the person to whom he is listening. There are even circumstances where the integrity is lacking and the good listener, by his respect for the other, can create it. In any event we are to remember that integrity, by definition, cannot be far from the Kingdom of God. And it is also worth remembering that in the very act of listening to the questions which the other man is asking we may grasp in a new way

[1] D. Webster, op. cit., pp. 58-9.

the very gospel with which we have been entrusted. His very difficulties enlarge our understanding of the range of the answer we are commissioned to provide. But first we must learn to listen.

But in learning to listen to those who have thought God out of existence, and for whom therefore the Cross has no meaning, we have by no means exhausted the range of our responsibilities in what we have called our post-Christian society. There are those, and there are many of them, who are not asking questions and do not appear to want any answers. These are the men and women, young and old, who have 'never had it so good' and whose only grumble is that it isn't getting better fast enough.

These are much more difficult for the Christian, for the evangelist, to understand until he realizes how much he has in common with them! For this materialism, this hedonism, which seems to mock every attempt at serious enquiry, is more of a mental climate than a fixed attitude to life. The shock of the world-wars, the haunting fear of another even more terrible one, and somewhere deep down the legacy of insecurity stemming from the economic disasters of the thirties—these have combined to create a climate of opinion, a mood which none of us can wholly escape. Because material good and sensual pleasure are so precarious, and yet paradoxically so easy to come by, we warm 'both hands before the fire of life' and are only fearful lest that fire should sink too soon, long, indeed, before we are ready to depart.[1]

Nothing is easier than to denounce such a materialistic attitude to life, to don the hair-shirt of the prophet and castigate the sins of the age. What is far more difficult, what is so rarely attempted, is to achieve that 'detachment from creatures' which is a positive asceticism. We have, at one and the same time, to have an ungrudging appreciation of the goodness of the whole material order while being free of its mastery. This is not to make a separation of the sacred

[1] See Walter Savage Landor's poem 'Finis'.

and the secular. Rather it calls for a true sacred secularity which honours the secular as the very sphere in which the sacred is defined. This means in practice learning how to say 'no' for the right reasons, lest we find ourselves too easily saying 'yes' for the wrong ones. The ramifications of such a spirit of detachment, if applied in the practice of living, will have some unexpected results for the Christian Church as well as for individual Christians.

There is a story from the life of St Francis which will illustrate this:

> Once, when Brother Peter saw that their Church of St Maria de Portiuncula was crowded by brethren from distant parts, and that the alms were not enough to provide them with necessaries, he applied to St Francis, saying: 'I know not what I am to do to provide for the needs of the brethren. I pray thee to allow somewhat of the property of novices entering the Order to be reserved so that recourse may be had to it in time of necessity.' The holy man would allow no such compromise. 'What am I to do then?' said Peter. 'Strip the Virgin's altar,' replied St Francis, 'and take away its various ornaments, since thou canst not help the needy in any other way. Believe me, she will be better pleased to have her Son's Gospel observed and her altar stript, than to have the altar vested and her Son despised. The Lord will send someone to restore to his Mother what He has lent us.'[1]

Perhaps within that story we can see the lineaments of the Cross as it has to be demonstrated within an affluent society before it can readily be preached to those who are its beneficiaries.

It is right that we should have dwelt first upon the task which confronts us of relating the Cross to post-Christian society, for we are as Christians part of it, sharing in its repudiation of that earlier society, the society which professed to be Christian, which at its best acknowledged the claims of the Gospel, and at its worst knew what the

[1] I have culled that story from Arthur Hopkinson's book. *Hope— The Reflections of an Optimist* (Constable 1929), pp. 126-7.

claims were even when it rejected them. In that earlier society Christ might be mocked, imprisoned, crucified, but his relevance was never doubted. As Christians we are committed, in relation to the post-Christian society, to being a perpetual memorial of Christ's death until he comes into his own again.

But there is another society, another world, which is in no sense post-Christian, for it has never acknowledged Christ at all, and to a very considerable extent has never heard of him, or if it has done so has heard but a bowdlerized version of his Gospel, seen his figure only in caricature. This is the world of those great religious-cultures which have never been baptized.

We are beginning very slowly to realize that as yet there has been no real encounter between the Christian Gospel and the religious-cultures of Hinduism and Buddhism. We are beginning to suspect that there are depths in the religious consciousness of the African which few white men, if any, have succeeded in exploring. And we know to our loss that from the very beginning Islam has rejected what it has only half understood.

Are we then to say that the story of the modern missionary enterprise from Francis Xavier to Albert Schweitzer has been a failure? Surely, no! But we have to understand what that missionary enterprise has done and what remains to do. What it has done has been to plant little Christian communities, and in a few places, quite large communities, in the very context of these alien religious-cultures. The real encounter, however, is still to come. For these 'colonies' have been planted under the aegis of an imperialism which is now in retreat.

The Hindu, the Buddhist, the Confucianist, the Shinto devotee, and those who have abandoned these systems of belief but have retained their cultural forms, all alike have seen Christianity fundamentally as an expression of cultural aggression, expressed too often with scant respect for their own sensibilities. They have much to forgive. That is something Christians need to remember when they seek to interpret the Gospel of forgiveness. It is not enough to know that God has forgiven us. We have to receive the forgiveness of these men of other Faiths. This will mean an interpretation of the Cross in our ministry of evangelism which it will be very hard to achieve. We can only seek forgiveness in the light of the universal relevance of the Cross. But how are we to convince the men of these other Faiths that we all meet at the Cross and that we want them to forgive us there? That is the essence of the encounter that lies ahead.

To understand this aright we must remember that, in the thinking of Asia and Africa, religion and life are all of a piece. To be a Christian is to be identified with the life of the West. It is part of the cross carried by the Indian and African, the Arab and Chinese Christian that the Christ of the Cross is not yet understood to have been Man. He is still resented and suspect as a white man.

Nevertheless, this is one world and has been so designed that all men may live in it together. No race can say of another 'I have no need of thee'. The argument of I Corinthians 12 is as relevant for the body of humanity as it is for the body of the Church. This points towards the continuation of the missionary task, whatever the colour of the missionary. For he is the prophet of the humanity that is to be. His very 'foreignness' is part of his Gospel for he is at home everywhere. That is his calling as he follows in the footsteps of the Son of Man. This does not mean that he will be accepted everywhere. '*As* the Father hath sent me, *even so* send I you' still stands in all its grandeur and its grimness as the commission of the missionary.

We have looked at the ministry of evangelism in relation to the post-Christian world. We have viewed the unfinished task in relation to the great faith-cultures of Asia and Africa. What is so disconcerting is to discover ever and again how many there are in our Churches who think they know who Jesus is, but who in their lack of charity to those who are without earn the rebuke of Jesus to his intolerant disciples, 'You do not know to what spirit you belong' (Luke 9.55). The episode in which those words occur is perhaps significant. Jesus was now setting his course directly to Jerusalem. St Luke is quite clear that Jesus knew what lay ahead. For St Luke, the Gentile, writing in retrospect, it was not without significance that on this last journey Jesus sought hospitality from Samaritans, a people who were strangers to the covenant of Israel, aliens like Luke himself. And the Samaritans refused to receive Jesus. The Cross was casting its shadow before here also, as so often in the ministry of Jesus. And then we get the reactions of two of the most intimate of Jesus' disciples who could only think of revenging the insult. We are still a long way in that story from the true encounter of the disciples of Jesus with those of another faith. It was to two devoted members of his own intimate circle that Jesus had to say, in response to their insensitivity to those outside, 'You do not know to what spirit you belong'. For it is of the very essence of the spirit of Jesus that he was outward-going in his living and his dying. For very many in our congregations there is need of a conversion experience, an experience not only of turning to Jesus but also of following him as he goes out beyond the congregation. Many have still to learn the truth of a remark of Archbishop William Temple when he said that 'The Church is the only society that exists for the benefit of those who are not its members'.

Meanwhile, whether it be the seekers or the satisfied of the post-Christian world; the suspicious adherents of the other religious faiths; or God's frozen people in the pews (and sometimes in the pulpits!); all alike are offended by the Cross. There is enough ugliness and pain in the world without making a symbol of it, so many think. Others want to see quick results and are utterly impatient with the patience of God. Yet others care only for a success story. And by the world's standards the Cross was not a success story at the first, and it is still not recognized as a success story. Only those who submit to its judgment and take it seriously discover in and through it the meaning of success.

We have, then, on any reckoning a formidable task to perform in our ministry of evangelism. In this, as in so many other respects, Canon Webster has a word of shrewd advice and substantial encouragement to give us. 'For large areas of modern evangelism there are,' he says, 'no precedents. But there is the Holy Ghost.'[1]

Because our modern world is so complex and the structures of power, as well as patterns of social life, so varied, the task of evangelism has to be envisaged in terms of a many-sided approach. The earliest expression of this many-sidedness of evangelism is found in I Corinthians, ch. 12. But it receives more succinct form in Ephesians where we read

. . . these were his gifts: some to be apostles, some prophets, some evangelists, some pastors and teachers, to equip God's people for work in his service. (Eph. 4.11-12)

In the relatively simple organization of the first-century Church certain gifts are noted. It would be a doubtful assumption to define the gifts as corresponding to offices. Already a diaconate to serve tables had produced one martyr, Stephen, and one extremely apostolic evangelist, Philip. We may legitimately assume that, in the passage in Ephesians, the gifts had a distinctive and not an exclusive significance. What is important to note is that *all* the gifts had one common purpose—'to equip God's people for work in his service'. This is the beginning of a many-sided evangelism.

But that same passage goes on to insist that, in addition to equipping God's people for his service, these same gifts are designed to 'build up the body of Christ'. It is as though, from the first, it was assumed that God's people could only effectively act in God's service against the background of a community life out of which their service sprang.

[1] Douglas Webster, op. cit., p. 75.

And that community life was itself defined in the most exalted terms possible. The community was to attain to a maturity of life 'measured by nothing less than the full stature of Christ' (Eph. 4.13).

The reason for this high calling of the Christian community is that introducing people to Jesus Christ does in practice involve introducing them to his people. That is normal experience. Canon Webster is not using hyperbole when he says:

> If we want to be evangelistically effective in the world of the outsider, it is crucial to do all in our power to see that Christ is the predominantly visible mark of the Church and that he is not imprisoned behind the walls of our ecclesiastical system.[1]

With that standard for our corporate life as Christians we go out from the Church into the world along a threefold path of action.

First in order of importance, because in this all can be involved, we go out to meet other people in a person-to-person encounter. This will certainly mean, sooner or later, giving a reason for the hope that is in us (I Peter 3.15). It is worth while setting this readiness to bear testimony to our faith within the whole context of the first Epistle of St Peter, which deals with Christians on the verge of persecution. It is a timely reminder that the Cross of Christ and the cross of the Christian are very closely linked in evangelism.

But the person-to-person encounter along the ordinary ways of daily life can also be an encounter between families. And in our present-day world the Christian family, the Christian home, may well prove to be the most powerful factor in evangelism we possess.

A home
Is the armoury of God
In His battle to the death with evil, cruelty, lust.

[1] Douglas Webster, op. cit., p. 56.

A home
Is a tool to be used by God
In His own mysterious working,
To bring friendship and joy to the lonely and despairing,
To lift off loads of grief,
To block the mouth of hell,
To fling wide the portals of Heaven.

A home
Is a treasury of God
Wherein purity, beauty and joy
Are stored, for His purposes, inviolate.

A home
Shall be potent
Through the world and beyond it
To scatter abroad the love and the knowledge of God.

For a home
Is in itself the triumph of God,
Banishing Night and Chaos and Necessity,
Indwelling this lifeless clay
With the spirit divine of freedom and joy
Overcoming to all eternity
Evil with Good.[1]

Second in order of importance in the circumstances of our day is the deliberate involvement of Christians in the whole fabric of social, industrial, civic and political life—the recognition that these are the frontiers where human life needs to be redeemed. For it is on these frontiers that man's thinking about himself and about his world is being shaped. It is at these points of strength and weakness in our modern society that men will discover God as relevant if they are to discover him at all. Here the Christian goes with virtually no precedents to assist him. No man has yet discovered how to live creatively and constructively on these new frontiers. What is certain is that somewhere and somehow the pattern

[1] J. S. Hoyland, *The Sacrament of Common Life—A Book of Devotion* (W. Heffer and Sons, Cambridge 1927), p. 61.

of the Cross will emerge. The horizontal bar will be a costly one, and the nails will be found to be sharp. But if life is to have meaning then it must have depth and that points towards the need of the vertical upon which the horizontal can be hung. The Christian's responsibility on these frontiers is to unveil the Cross in its relevance to modern life. Only then will we be wise to talk about it.

The *third* pattern of action, only valid today if the other two patterns are also being followed by the Christian Church, is through the word of interpretation proclaimed through the books and art and all the mass media of our time. Only if the first two patterns of activity are being worked effectively will there be anything to be interpreted. But if they are being worked in this way then the word of interpretation will be listened to. The word of the Cross will be found to be the Wisdom of God, but only if the condition is fulfilled. Today, demonstration must come first, and essentially it must be the demonstration of a living community. For it is the lack of any real sense of belonging which is the twentieth-century crisis of man.

There is a passage in St Paul's second letter to the Corinthians which can bring this particular argument to a point from which a new start can be made. He has been speaking about the Cross as the place where men can discover that they belong to God and to one another. A new world swims into our ken. There, with great humility and yet boldness, he sketches in the character of the evangelizing community of the Cross:

In order that our service may not be brought into discredit, we avoid giving offence in anything. As God's servants, we try to recommend ourselves in all circumstances by our steadfast endurance: in hardships and dire straits; flogged, imprisoned, mobbed; overworked, sleepless, starving. We recommend ourselves by the innocence of our behaviour, our grasp of truth, our patience and kindliness; by gifts of the Holy Spirit, by sincere love, by declaring the truth, by the power of God. We wield the weapons of assurance can be communicated. They are designed to satisfy a fundamental human need, a need which is not limited to childhood. They are the very beautiful and meaningful testimonies to the Mother-heart of God, to the imaginative sensitiveness of the God-Man, Christ Jesus, *and* to the imaginative obedience of his immediate disciples who were quite clear about his intention with regard to both Baptism and Holy Communion, and who handed down to us the privilege and responsibility of continuing the same.

God, in his creative purpose for our good, intends us to be whole men and women, integrated personalities, in whom both conscious and unconscious are in harmony. This is that wholeness which is health. But we are, in fact, sick. We need healing. We need that integration of personality which we know we do not possess. The sacraments of the Gospel in their several ways minister to our healing not least by their activity in preventing us escaping from the fact of our sickness. Would we banish the memory of unpleasant experiences, the thoughts we fear, the challenges we wish to evade, imprisoning them in our 'unconsciousness'? The sacraments of the Gospel, properly understood and faithfully received, prevent us from such an escape which would, if permitted, make our healing impossible.

The sacraments of Baptism and the Holy Communion do this in simple and direct fashion by presenting us with the Cross in all its potent symbolism. These sacraments in their very simplest form are *aides-mémoire*, instruments for recalling to our minds what we so easily forget. They are much more than aids to memory. But in a deeply fundamental way they are that and we must rejoice in them as such. Luther, when almost overwhelmed by the assaults of evil, and by his own doubts and uncertainties, would exclaim *'baptizatus sum'*. He recalled the objective fact of his baptism. But, in that recalling, he did not only remember that he had been baptized. He looked at the inwardness of baptism, at what God did there; linked directly as God's doing there was what God had done long before in the baptism of

righteousness in right hand and left. Honour and dishonour, praise and blame, are alike our lot: we are the impostors who speak the truth, the unknown men whom all men know; dying we still live on; disciplined by suffering, we are not done to death; in our sorrows we have always cause for joy; poor ourselves, we bring wealth to many; penniless, we own the world. (II Cor. 6.3-10)

8

The Cross in the Sacraments
of the Gospel

IN THE Introduction to his commentary on the book
Leviticus, Dr Nathaniel Micklem has this important ob-
servation in regard to our understanding of the meaning of
the word 'sacrifice' as it applies in the most solemn rites of
religious worship. Writing of the religion of the Hebrew
people as we have it in the Old Testament he says:

> We do great injustice to the sacrificial worship of Israel if
> we regard it as a form of primitive magic. Sacrifice is perhaps
> older than vocal prayer; it *is* prayer in its simplest and still
> inarticulate form. An infant stretches out its arms to its
> mother long before it can speak with words; but the stretch-
> ing out of the arms is eloquence and prayer; it is not magic.[1]

Coupled with that quotation I would like to put this incident
recorded by the late Dr D. M. Baillie in his book *The
Theology of the Sacraments*. The passage runs:

> Some years ago I heard a woman lecturer on child psy-
> chology say something which immediately seemed to me to
> have a bearing on sacramental doctrine. She was speaking of
> a hospital for motherless babies in India, and how, for lack
> of a mother, many of the babies pined away and died, how-
> ever well-fed and attended. The nurses, of course, kept the
> usual rule of not handling the babies unnecessarily, but let-
> ting them lie in their cots with a regular routine and the

[1] Nathaniel Micklem, *The Book of Leviticus*, The Interpreter's
Bible (Abingdon Press, New York and Nashville, USA 1953), Vol.
II, p. 12.

> minimum of interference. But one day, she told us, an
> Indian woman walking about the ward and dandling a baby
> in her arms said, 'Why don't you let the nurses dandle the
> babies? *A baby must have love.*' The lecturer went on to
> explain how nothing can take the place of that physical way
> of communicating affection, the maternal touch, the actual
> loving contact of the mother's or the foster-mother's hand
> with the baby's body—'epidermis against epidermis', and not
> for any purely physical reasons, but because 'a baby must
> have love', and only through that subconscious channel can
> the maternal love reach a child who has not yet any self-
> conscious existence at all.[1]

In launching thus upon our voyage of understanding our
expedition of discovery into the meaning of the two great
sacraments of the Gospel, Baptism and Holy Communion,
and their relation to the Cross, I have done so for the simple
reason that we need to know why the sacraments were
instituted before we can fully enter into their meaning, and
enjoy their relevance.

The two quotations, the one from Dr Micklem and the
one from Dr Baillie, have this in common, that they both
give us the picture of the child reaching out for love. They
remind us of what we so very easily forget, that, in thinking
about the God whom we worship, we must think not only of
the Father-love of God but also of the Mother-love of God.
'God created man in his own image, in the image of God
he created him; male and female he created them' (Gen
1.27, RSV). That ancient insight into human nature and into
the nature of God has, in our day, found interesting con-
firmation in the researches of those who explore the deep
places of man's 'unconscious'. Poets and artists have always
been aware of this, and the writer of the book Genesis is
indubitably a poet and artist. In every man there is woman,
in every woman man. In the image of God created he them.
The sacraments of the Gospel speak, then, to our need of
love, for intimacy, for the tangible through which love

[1] Donald M. Baillie, op. cit. (Faber and Faber 1957), pp. 8

Jesus. In recalling 'the water of rebirth' (Titus 3.5), which is what baptism signifies, Luther, and how many others since his time, not least ourselves, brought himself, as we bring ourselves, into the light—the light of God's redemptive purpose, love and action. All God's goodness and all our badness are in the light together. In reminding ourselves about ourselves, and accepting ourselves as ourselves, we discover that we are accepted. There is profound psychological wisdom in saying *'baptizatus sum'* if we know and mean what we say.

More vividly still is such a remembering provided for in the Holy Communion. We hold that the first disciples were right in believing that Christ, our Lord, 'did institute, and in his holy Gospel command us to continue a perpetual memorial of that his precious death'.

Far more frequently, in a way not possible in the unrepeatable sacrament of baptism, we do at the Holy Communion remember again the crucified Saviour and why it was that he went of his own loving free-will to be crucified.

The Holy Communion is designed, among its many other purposes, to bring us to ourselves, to bring our total selves out into the light of God's healing, integrating, love. This totality of ourselves is something we so easily forget. Indeed, some forms of sacramental devotion tend to encourage us to forget it, to forget that we are not alone with our Lord when we eat the bread and drink from the cup. At that very moment the profoundest truth of what we do is that we are sharing in a common experience—'We, many as we are, are one body; for it is one loaf of which we all partake.' Holy Communion means Holy Community or it is neither Communion nor Holy. Christ died for me, yes: but that is true only because he died for all humanity of which I am one unit. His 'one oblation of himself once offered' was 'for the sins of the whole world'. I share in a universal redemption or I am not redeemed at all.

Once again, the discoveries being made about our unconscious selves shed great light on this aspect of the Holy

Communion. We are learning to think of a 'collective un-conscious', a whole realm which we share in common with *all* mankind. It is at that tremendously deep level that the all-sufficient sacrifice of Calvary *satisfies*. (I would make clear that in using that word 'satisfies' I intend a far wider range of meaning than is comprised under the use of the word 'satisfaction' in the traditional penitential language of the Church.)

The sacraments of Baptism and Holy Communion speak to us, then, under simple guise, of the Mother-love and the Father-love of God. Each in its special way, through the use of material things, matches our need for love, is at once intimate and tangible, is the outward and visible *medium* through which an inward and spiritual grace can be com-municated.

We must, however, seek to penetrate beyond these great simplicities which indicate how these two sacraments match our human need. For all too easily we judge our needs by superficial standards. We do not realize how needy we truly are. To this end we need to stretch our minds and, in refreshing our own memories, to 'make memorial' of our Lord's own Baptism and of what he did at the Last Supper.

What was it that brought Jesus to the Jordan river to be baptized of John? That question forces itself upon us as we reflect on two facts—one, the consistent testimony of the New Testament that our Lord, despite the severest and subtlest temptations, never swerved from the divine will. Positively, he was so preoccupied with obedience that he did not disobey. Yet John's baptism, so it is stated, was explicitly a 'baptism of repentance' (Luke 3.3, RSV). The second fact is that of the puzzling word of Jesus to John when John pro-tested at Jesus coming to be baptized—'Let it be so for the present: we do well to conform in this way with all that God requires.' That is how the New English Bible renders the more familiar Authorized Version of Matthew 3.15. 'Suffer it to be so now: for thus it becometh us to fulfil all righteousness.'

One sensitive commentator has suggested some reasons why Jesus came to John and received baptism at his hands.

Jesus would have heard of the moral awakening which was one result of John's preaching. What more natural, remembering his kinship with John, than that Jesus should want to go and identify himself with this ministry, giving to John the support of his fellowship?

May it not also have been a fact that the spiritual movement taking place in the lives of so many, something that looked like being a mass movement, should have been a sign to Jesus that the time for his own public ministry had come? At least we do know that it was from the time of his Baptism that his public ministry did in fact begin.

Where would that public ministry end? In meditating upon his calling, Jesus being a man profoundly versed in the long record of his people's great prophets and the results of their ministries, must have asked himself that question. For him, so it is suggested, there was the possibility of a subtle sin, 'the sin of shrinking from what might lie ahead, the conceivable sin of the lower rather than the higher choice'. He would be baptized, therefore, not for repentance but for the utter consecration of being completely ready.

The fourth suggested reason is that Jesus never thought of himself in isolation. His sympathy with the needs of his people prompted him always to identification with them. 'He was a son of Israel, and all that belonged to his people in heritage as well as in hope he took upon himself. Vicariously, therefore, he would be baptized into their need for repentance, and with them and for them express the urgency of commitment to the Kingdom of God.'[1]

Because Jesus was a man living in a particular nation at a particular moment in its history it is wholly legitimate to believe, from all that we know of him, that such motives would have brought him that day to the banks of the

[1] Walter Russell Bowie, *The Gospel according to St Luke*, Interpreter's Bible, Vol. VIII, p. 78.

Jordan, would have made him overrule the protests of John and go down into the water.

What did that going down into the water mean to Jesus? What did he experience in that going down and coming up? That is our question now and our reserve in attempting to answer it must be strict. How difficult it is to estimate even fractionally the inwardness of another person's experience, even of someone intimately related and greatly beloved. Our unconscious may indeed be 'a peece of the *Continent,* a part of the *Maine*' as John Donne says. 'No man is an Iland, intire of itself.'[1] True enough, and it is a most weighty truth, to be accepted and explored. Yet, nevertheless, the conscious mind of man knows loneliness. And there is a loneliness, an aloneness, which our respect for personality demands that we should not attempt to penetrate. We must wait on revelation. We cannot compel it. Of such was the aloneness of the baptism experience of Jesus. Only what he himself revealed can we with any propriety seek to understand. And he did reveal enough to make it quite clear that for him the Baptism in Jordan was an anticipation of the Cross. Before we consider two passages which certainly link his Baptism with the Cross it may be helpful, in the light of what we have already seen of the universal relevance of the sacrifice of Christ, to consider the words of a great contemporary scholar.

Dr Cullmann writes:

> All men have in principle received Baptism long ago, namely on Golgotha, at Good Friday and Easter. There the essential act of Baptism was carried out, entirely without our co-operation, and even without our faith. There the whole world was baptized on the ground of the absolutely sovereign act of God, who in Christ 'first loved us' (I John 4.19) before we loved him, even before we believed.[2]

---

[1] *John Donne, Dean of St Paul's—Complete Poetry and Selected Prose,* edited by John Hayward (The Nonsuch Press, London and New York 1941), p. 538.
[2] Oscar Cullmann, *Baptism in the New Testament* (SCM Press 1950), p. 23.

If Christians are right in their belief about the universal relevance of the work of Jesus Christ, then what Cullmann says is of the highest significance for the 'collective unconscious' of mankind. Here, to use Jung's phraseology, is a potential 'archetype' of enormous importance for the Christian witness to the Gospel, for our ministry of evangelism. For if this is true then we may make use of another Jungian phrase which has been adopted from the primitive psychology of the Naskapi Indians of Labrador. These Indians speak of 'the inborn Great Man, who lives in each one of us'.[1] We may venture beyond the psychologists and believe that this 'Great Man in the heart', whose full revelation is said to be man made perfect, is none other than the Man Christ Jesus. That, of course, is an act of faith. But if the Baptism of Jesus has the significance which Dr Cullmann, following the New Testament, says that it has, then our understanding of it prepares us for what he has to say himself and so points us towards a new and deeper insight into what baptism should mean for ourselves.

So we turn to two brief sayings of Jesus. The first is recorded in Mark 10.38, 'Can you drink the cup that I drink, or be baptized with the baptism I am baptized with?' Dr Robinson, after pointing out that in St Mark the verbs are in the present tense—'the baptism that I am being baptized with', 'the cup that I am drinking', goes on to say:

> The baptism of Jesus is his whole existence in the form of a servant, all that is included in his being upon earth 'not to be ministered unto but to minister, and to give his life a ransom for many' (Mark 10.45).[2]

To this may be added some other words of Dr Cullmann dealing with the Baptism of Jesus in the Jordan,

[1] *Man and his Symbols*, edited by Carl G. Jung and, after his death, M.-L. von Franz (Aldus Books, London 1964), pp. 161-2.
[2] J. A. T. Robinson, 'The One Baptism as a category of New Testament Soteriology', an article in *The Scottish Journal of Theology*, Vol. 6, No. 3, September 1953, p. 259.

Other Jews came to Jordan to be baptized by John for their *own* sins. Jesus, on the contrary, at the very moment when he is baptized like other people hears a voice which fundamentally declares: *Thou* art baptized not for *thine own* sins but for those of the whole people. For thou art he of whom Isaiah prophesied, that he must suffer representatively for the sins of the people. This means that Jesus is baptized in view of his death, which effects forgiveness of sins for all men.[1]

Those two quotations send us back to the picture of the suffering servant of Isaiah 53. It is hard not to believe that in the consciousness of Jesus there must have been a steadily growing awareness of his own identity with the figure of Isaiah 53, an awareness which would have begun at his Baptism and grown with every day of his earthly ministry. If that be so, then there is a direct link between what he experienced in his Baptism and what he endured upon the Cross *and* upon everything in between. For always he was among men as the suffering servant.

What is important for us to note is, that after the sons of Zebedee, little knowing what they were saying, had replied to Jesus' question with a 'Yes, we are able,' Jesus quietly puts his and their present into his and their future, 'The cup that I am drinking you shall drink; and the baptism I am being baptized with shall be your baptism.' But this in fact proved to be true only after the actual event of crucifixion.

This brings us to the second of these brief sayings of Jesus which occurs in Luke 12.50, 'I have a baptism to undergo, and how hampered I am until the ordeal is over!' Once again the Greek is illuminating. The Greek rendered by the words 'until the ordeal is over', *heōs hotou telesthē*, foreshadows the cry from the Cross 'it is finished', *tetelestai*. To quote Dr Robinson again,

Until the baptism is thoroughly finished . . . the Son of Man is straitened; it is only in the Cross and Resurrection that its confinement to Jesus' person is broken.[2]

[1] Oscar Cullmann, op. cit., p. 18.
[2] J. A. T. Robinson, op. cit., p. 260.

After the crucifixion at Calvary and only after that crucifixion can we share in his Baptism. But then we do share in it. The great argument of St Paul in Romans 6 is as explicit as possible:

Have you forgotten that when we were baptized into union with Christ Jesus we were baptized into his death? By baptism we were buried with him, and lay dead, in order that as Christ was raised from the dead in the splendour of the Father, so also we might set our feet upon the new path of life. (Rom. 6.3-4)

The sacrament of Baptism is *a sacrament of death*, of a daily dying, which becomes effective for each one of us because once, in complete perfection, the sacrament was lived out in a dying life whose symbol is the Cross.

All this is comprised in our refusal to acquiesce in the world's slow stain, in our patience amid the uncertainties and perplexities of faith, which we must experience if we would prove the truth and be set free by it, as well as in our resistance to the assaults of evil—all this is comprised in our defiance when we say, '*baptizatus sum*'.

In seeking to 'make memorial' of our Lord's Baptism we have sought to learn from his words and from his life something of what that Baptism meant for him, and what our baptism can mean for us. How can we best 'make memorial' of what he did at the Last Supper?

That is no easy question to answer. We do indeed 'make memorial' every time we obey what we are satisfied was his command, 'This do in remembrance of me'. There is a variety of ways in which that memorial is made, but wherever the intention is to do what our Lord commanded we may be confident of the blessing of his sacramental presence.

And we must never underestimate the importance of this memorial, for we have seen something of its profound psychological significance. Nor should we minimize the physical reality of the sacred elements. These 'creatures of bread and wine' are his 'creatures', his created means by which we can, as in a mystery, be reached by his love. They are pledges, symbols, signs which are profoundly effective, not just to our conscious minds but, more important still, in the depths of our unconscious.

Yet, that being said, we must ask ourselves the question— 'What was it that our Lord had in mind at the Last Supper?' Is the meaning exhausted by the brilliantly contrived psychology of so dramatic a sacrament, and the means thus provided to save us from all false attempts to escape from ourselves and to evade the challenges of life? Is it even exhausted by its rich symbolism of self-giving love, its power to conjure up a readiness for self-sacrifice on our part? Reverently we may believe that all this was in his mind. Certainly it has proved to be all this for multitudes.

But the sacrament means more than this. If in the living and dying of Jesus we see God reconciling the world to himself (II Cor. 5.19), then we must believe that in the deepest sense the risen and ascended Christ is now representing Man in the very heart of God—Man perfect *and* men to be perfected, himself as Man, ourselves as men. He is our representative before the throne. Mysteriously he is our representative on the throne.

Was this also part of what he intended when he did what he did in the Upper Room? May it be that the answer lies somewhere in the mystery of the Sacrament of Holy Communion, seen not primarily as a ritual occasion of worship so much as the ritual expression of a life of obedience? The Sacrament of Holy Communion is a *Sacrament of life*.

In and through the Sacrament Christ comes to us and lives to us. And who is this Christ? It is the Christ who in perfect obedience to his Father's will offered himself in an offering in which the obedience of a perfect life was consummated in the obedience of a perfect death. So he comes to us, but not only to us who are in his body the Church. He comes to all humanity. He is present in all humanity. For his redemptive love was all-prevailing. And wherever, and in whatever form, man obey's God's loving purposes there is the Christ in that man's obedience.

Professor Moule has developed this insight most movingly in his chapter on 'The Eucharistic Sacrifice' which concludes his little book, *The Sacrifice of Christ*. Writing of Christ's once-and-for-all sacrifice being implemented in us he says:

> And every Eucharist is a 'focal' point of that; not a mere recalling to the mind, nor yet a re-enactment; but an entering into what Christ has done—just as indeed is every symbol of obedience.[1]

To enter into what Christ has done is to enter into his own sacrificial obedience. Instead of pleading the sacrifice we become part of it. It is in this context that Professor Moule quotes from Archbishop Temple these memorable words:

> The Eucharist is a sacrifice; but we do not offer it; Christ offers it; and we, responding to his act, take our parts or shares in his own sacrifice as members of his body. The bread which the Church, by the hands of the priest, breaks and gives is the Body of Christ, that is, it is the Church itself. . . . Christ in us presents us with himself to the Father; we in him yield ourselves to be so presented; or, to put it in other words, Redeeming love so wins our hearts that we offer ourselves to be presented by the Love that redeems to the Love that created and sustains both us and all the universe.[2]

Somewhere here is to be found the inner significance of those strange words recorded in each of the Synoptic Gospels as being said by our Lord when at the Last Supper he instituted the Sacrament of Holy Communion.

> I tell you this: never again shall I drink from the fruit of the vine until that day when I drink it new in the Kingdom of my Father. (Mark 14.25; cf. Matt. 26.29 and Luke 22.16 and 18)

Deliberately, so it seems, our Lord set the very action by

[1] C. F. D. Moule, op. cit. (Hodder and Stoughton 1956), p. 54.
[2] William Temple, *Christus Veritas—An Essay* (Macmillan and Co. 1926), pp. 241-2.

which he took the bread and broke it, took the wine and blessed it, within the context of something that was still to happen, the coming Kingdom of God, which he was to inaugurate by his death. It is important for Christian thinking that we remember that the phrase 'The Kingdom of God' on the lips of Jesus meant at once an eternal reality, a present experience *and* a future hope. It is not always easy to discern which of these meanings is the governing one in any particular instance. No doubt it is true that whenever he used the words he had all three meanings in mind. But at least on this occasion, when he was instituting the Sacrament of Holy Communion, the accent must have lain upon 'the future hope'.

Surely we may hazard the view that what was wholly concerning him at that moment was nothing less than the fulness of the Kingdom, that fulness which would be the fulness of recognition and acceptance of God's rule. He had said earlier, so the fourth Gospel tells us, 'I shall draw all men to myself, when I am lifted up from the earth.' And the writer makes clear that, 'This he said to indicate the kind of death he was to die' (John 12.32-33). There would seem to be no convincing reason for imagining that, in fact, Jesus thought that his death would bring history to an end. What we may believe is that he did himself believe that his death would be a revelation of what the God who rules is like. Nor was he disappointed, for as subsequent history demonstrates Christians have, by faith, seen that at the Cross 'God was in Christ'.

But it would also seem to have been in the mind of Jesus that this revelation must be re-presented before the eyes of men, both as an assurance of what the Cross revealed and as a promise of what was to come, and also as a means of living in the present. This at least is certain that the earliest Christian tradition of which we have knowledge, a tradition many years older than the earliest Gospel, so interpreted the mind of Christ. Writing to the Church of Corinth in the year A.D. 51 Paul can say:

For the tradition which I handed on to you came to me from the Lord himself: that the Lord Jesus, on the night of his arrest, took bread and, after giving thanks to God, broke it and said: 'This is my body, which is for you; do this as a memorial of me.' In the same way, he took the cup after supper, and said: 'This cup is the new covenant sealed by my blood. Whenever you drink it, do this as a memorial of me.'

And Paul adds:

For every time you eat this bread, and drink the cup, you proclaim the death of the Lord, until he comes. (I Cor. 11. 23-26)

We have earlier seen how, elsewhere in the same letter, the apostle makes clear to these same Christians that to eat the bread and drink the wine is to share in the life of the Christ himself, who lives not only in the splendour of God but also in the very far from splendid community which is his Church.

If Paul was accurately reporting what had been handed down to him by those who were present at the Last Supper: if subsequent Christian experience has most fully proved the truth of the experience communicated through this Sacrament: then we are justified in claiming that in the Upper Room, on the night of his arrest, Jesus was looking forward, looking into a future whose distances, at the time, his mind could not measure, and providing for his disciples, then and now, bread for each day's need, a very means of life, our *viaticum*, our provision for the road.

The road is a long one. Did our Lord ever imagine it would be short? 'Drawing all men to himself' could scarcely be the work of a day or a week or a year, or even of a generation. Again, we may believe, his Apostle Paul had a true insight when he saw all creation 'waiting', waiting 'for God's sons to be revealed' (Rom. 8.19). But even that revelation, and it has not been accomplished yet, would only be preparatory to the whole universe being seen to be the realm of God, 'all in heaven and on earth brought into a unity in Christ' (Eph. 1.10). That is the wide prospect, the great hope, of which the Sacrament of Holy Communion is a pre-figuration, a promise and a pledge.

For our encouragement we need these large views of Grace. They cannot be too large. But they are meant to stimulate our obedience in the commonplaces of life when often we cannot see more than one step ahead. The Sacrament of Holy Communion is meant to hold the Cross before our eyes in the routines of life, and not only in the moments when we catch sight of the 'delectable mountains'. It is with the here and now that the Gospel is concerned when it reiterates in such different contexts the command of Christ 'Follow me'. It is with the here and now that the collect for Palm Sunday sets before us 'the example of his great humility'.

'It is theologically false', says Professor Moule, 'to segregate the Gospel sacraments . . . from all those quasi-sacramental "focal" points of obedience in life—the tangible, datable implementations of our will to serve God. . . . Every time a Christian or a group of Christians does something for the Lord's sake, whether it is (positively) giving a donation of blood at a transfusion centre, or going to a house to visit someone in need, or rendering some service as a community; or whether (negatively) it is refusing some pleasure because it appears to hinder the Lord's work; and whether it is an external action or a secret transaction of the soul—at all such points the stream of the sacrifice of Calvary is still seen flowing. It is (if guardedly, we use a dichotomy of language) the Lord's obedience in us being offered up to God.'[1]

So the sacraments of the Gospel, themselves sacraments of the grace of Calvary, can, if we will allow them, flow out to irrigate the whole of the world's life. This, in sacramental terms, is the wisdom of the Cross.

[1] C. F. D. Moule, op. cit., p. 55.

INDEX OF NAMES

Baillie, D. M., 112, 113
Bowie, Walter Russell, 117
Browning, Robert, 31, 54f, 56
Bultmann, Rudolf, 54, 56, 63

Campbell, John McLeod, 23
Cranfield, C. E. B., 83
Cullmann, Oscar, 118, 119, 120

Dodd, C. H., 32
Donne, John, 36, 118
Drake, Francis, 31

Elijah, 95
Ezekiel, 91

Forsyth, P. T., 38, 39
Francis, St, 103
Franz, M.-L. von, 119
Freud, S., 76
Fromm, Eric, 27

Habakkuk, 48ff, 51, 53
Herbert, George, 48
Hezekiah, 46, 59
Hopkinson, Arthur, 103
Hosea, 15
Hoyland, J. S., 108f

Isaiah, 21, 36, 52, 59, 91, 120

James, William, 53
Jeffreys, M. C. V., 86f
Jung, C. G., 76, 119

Kennedy, G. Studdert, 92f
Kipling, Rudyard, 42ff

Landor, Walter Savage, 102
Luke, St, 72, 106

Luther, Martin, 114

Mackintosh, H. R., 39, 40
MacLeod, Fiona, 71, 80
Macmillan, Harold, 34
Manson, T. W., 88, 89, 92, 94
Maugham, Somerset, 57, 58, 59,
    60
Micaiah, 91
Micklem, Nathaniel, 112, 113
Morgan, Charles, 58
Moule, C. F. D., 62, 123, 126

Napier, B. D., 45
Neill, Stephen, 22, 23

Paul, St, 11, 17, 18, 23, 33, 36,
    37, 50, 54, 67, 78, 79, 95, 96,
    99, 110, 121, 124, 125
Philip the Evangelist, 52, 107

Robinson, J. A. T., 119, 120

Schweitzer, Albert, 29, 104
Shakespeare, William, 27, 58
Stephen, St, 107

Temple, William, 24, 106, 123
Tillich, Paul, 87
Tournier, Paul, 30, 31, 76
Toynbee, Arnold, 42

Waugh, Evelyn, 56
Webster, Douglas, 100, 101, 107,
    108
Weil, Simone, 29
West, Charles C., 47
Wilson, Colin, 100

Xavier, Francis, 104

INDEX OF NEW TESTAMENT REFERENCES

Matthew
3.15,   116
5.23-24,   29
7.11,   14
8.20,   82
10.20,   89
10.23,   94
11.19,   94
11.20-27,   90
11.28,   83
12.40,   94
12.50,   96
13.41,   94
16.9,   82
ch.25,   29
26.29,   123

Mark
3.20,   81
4.11-12,   82, 84
7.18,   82
8.34,   95
8.34-35,   64
10.38,   119
10.45,   119
14.25,   123
14.36,   70, 89

Luke
2.49-51,   81
3.3,   116
9.55,   106
10.17-22,   90
12.50,   120
14.27, 33,   64
17.10,   30
21.26,   11
22.16,   123
23.46-48,   72
24.21,   72

John
1.14,   17
1.18,   17
3.2,   82
3.16,   25
3.19,   63
3.36,   24

4.34,   70
6.38,   70
11.16,   95
12.26,   90
12.32,   71
12.32-33,   124
19.19,   72

Acts
2.22-24, 38-39,   96
8.34,   52
17.18,   96

Romans
ch.1,   18
1.21-24,   45
2.1-5,   18, 19
3.18,   11
ch.5,   78
5.8,   33
5.15,   36
5.20,   33
6.1-11,   78
6.3-4,   121
ch.7,   76
7.24,   36
8.19,   125
8.22,   67
8.23,   67
11.32,   19

I Corinthians
1.9,   80
1.10,   79
1.18-2.10,   9f
1.23-24,   99
11.23-26,   125
ch.12,   107
12.26,   18
15.58,   53

II Corinthians
1.5,   95
5.17,   37
5.19,   38, 54, 122
5.21,   23, 70
6.3-10,   110f

Galatians
2.20,   38, 53
6.1-2,   79

Ephesians
1.1,   38
1.7-8,   53
1.9,   53
1.10,   35, 126
2.12,   45
4.11-12,   107
4.13,   108

Philippians
ch.2,   13
3.10,   99

Colossians
1.15,   17
1.21-23,   67f
1.24,   95, 99
1.27,   67

Titus
3.5,   115

Hebrews
2.15,   54, 62
2.17,   70
2.18,   74
4.15-16,   94
5.8-9,   74
12.2,   71, 85

I Peter
2.21,   74
3.15,   108

II Peter
3.13,   22

I John
2.2,   65
3.14,   65
3.17,   86
4.20,   86

Revelation
21.24-26,   35